Presented To:

_____

From:

_____

Date:

_____

The Christmas Cookie Cookbook

2nd Printing

The Christmas Cookie Cookbook
ISBN 1-57757-015-4
Copyright © 1997 by Trade Life Book
P. O. Box 55325
Tulsa, Oklahoma 74155

Introduction

C	is for cookies!
H	is for the helpers!
R	is for recipes worth keeping!
I	is for imagination!
S	is for serving and snacking!
T	is for tasty and tasting!
M	is for mouth-watering goodness!
A	is for after-dinner treats!
S	is for the smiles and the scents of Christmas!

Flour flying, sugar sprinkling, eyes twinkling, tastebuds tingling! Nothing says "Merry Christmas!" quite as nicely as a platter heaping with homemade Christmas cookies! Written with you and yours in mind, this cookbook is filled with make-the-season-merry recipes, easy-to-bake cookies, and easy-to-implement ideas for making your Christmas kitchen heartwarming and cheery! Bursting with mouth-watering Christmas cookie recipes, plus fun tips and hints on ways to enjoy them! Everyone who enjoys holiday celebrations, the sights, smells, and sounds of Christmas baking, will enjoy this little book of tastes and tips.

Savor it!

Triple Chocolate Treats

Remember, Christmas is a time for sharing and celebrating with those who are most dear to us.

2	sticks butter or margarine, softened to room temperature	1/2	teaspoon salt
		3/4	teaspoon baking soda
1/2	cup sugar	1	12-ounce package white chocolate chips
1/2	cup firmly packed brown sugar	2	2-ounce squares white chocolate
1	large egg, beaten	2	2-ounce squares semisweet chocolate
2	teaspoons grated orange peel		
2 1/4	cups all-purpose flour		

Preheat oven to 350°. In large bowl, cream butter and sugars, with mixer on medium, until light. Beat in egg and orange peel. Combine flour, salt, and baking soda. Add a little at a time, with mixer on low, to creamed mixture, just until blended. Stir in white chocolate chips. Drop by the teaspoon, 2 inches apart, onto greased cookie sheets. Bake for 10 to 12 minutes or until golden. Use spatula to place cookies on wire racks to cool. When cool, place cookies on waxed paper. Melt white chocolate squares in microwave. Stir until smooth. Melt semisweet chocolate in a separate bowl. Place melted chocolate in separate pastry bags. Decorate tops of cookies with white chocolate, then semisweet chocolate. Set aside until chocolate sets. Makes about 60 cookies.

Sugar Bear Paws!

3/4	cup sugar
2	sticks butter (1 cup), softened to room temperature
2 1/2	cups all-purpose flour
1/4	cup ground pecans or almonds
	Confectioners' sugar

Cream sugar and butter together in mixing bowl. Stir in flour and nuts until mixture is well blended. Wrap dough in plastic wrap or waxed paper and chill for at least 1 hour. Preheat oven to 350°. Using buttered madeline (shell-shaped) pans, press 2 tablespoons of dough into each shape. Bake for 15 to 20 minutes or until lightly browned. Immediately remove from pans and roll or sprinkle tops and bottoms with confectioners' sugar. Let cool.

Makes 4 dozen.

Christmas cookies are the perfect gift for those special people who seem to have everything! They don't have your cookies!!!

Christmas Wreaths

Include Christmas cookies with your next "Care Package" to someone far away!

1/2	cup confectioners' sugar
1/2	cup cornstarch
1	cup all-purpose flour
1 1/2	sticks butter* (3/4 cup), softened to room temperature
	Christmas sprinkles or red and green sugars

Combine sugar, cornstarch, and flour in mixing bowl. Mix in butter until well blended. Divide mixture into 2 balls and chill for 45 minutes or until firm. Preheat oven to 300°. Roll 1 ball of dough out on a floured surface to a 9-inch diameter. Place on greased cookie sheet. With a small glass or cookie cutter, cut out center of circle, then gently cut the wreath into 10 to 12 wedge-shaped pieces. Place the pieces about 1 inch apart. Cover with sprinkles or sugars. Repeat for remaining dough. Bake for 18 to 22 minutes or until golden brown. Cool in pan for 5 minutes; place on wire rack to cool completely. To serve, place on serving platters in wreath shapes.

Makes 20 to 24 servings.

*Margarine should not be substituted.

Christmas Sugar Snowdrops!

1	cup sugar
2	sticks (1 cup) butter or margarine, softened to room temperature
1/2	teaspoon almond extract
1/2	teaspoon vanilla extract
1	egg, lightly beaten
2	cups all-purpose flour
1/2	cup finely chopped pecans or walnuts
	Sugar

Cream sugar and butter in mixing bowl. Add extracts and egg; beat until fluffy. Beat in flour and nuts until mixture is lightly moistened. Chill for 1 hour or until dough is easily handled. Preheat oven to 350°. Shape dough into 1-inch balls. Place on greased cookie sheet, 2 inches apart. Using a flat-bottomed glass, dip glass into sugar, then press balls to a 1/4-inch thickness. Sprinkle with more sugar, if desired. Bake for 10 to 12 minutes or until cookies are lightly golden.

Makes 3 dozen.

Make a Christmas cookie wreath! Hot glue cookies on a cardboard ring. Alternate colors and types, slightly overlay cookies around the circle. Polish it off with varnish or lacquer. Spray and attach a festive ribbon!

Christmas Cherry Winks

When sending that care package, cover your cookies with wax paper then pack them with popcorn to keep them from breaking.

1/2	cup cocoa	1	egg
1 1/2	cups all-purpose flour	1 1/2	teaspoons vanilla extract
1/4	teaspoon baking powder	1	10-ounce jar maraschino
1/4	teaspoon baking soda		cherries
1/4	teaspoon salt	1	6-ounce package semisweet
1	stick butter or margarine, softened to room temperature		chocolate chips
		1/2	cup sweetened condensed milk
1	cup sugar	4	teaspoons cherry juice

Preheat oven to 350°. In a large bowl, combine first 5 ingredients; set aside. In a large bowl, cream butter and sugar with mixer on medium. Add egg and vanilla, mixing well; add dry ingredients, a little at a time until well blended. Form dough into 1-inch balls. Place on ungreased cookie sheet. Press down center of dough with thumb and place a cherry in center. Bake for 10 minutes. Use spatula to place cookies on wire rack to cool. When cool, place wire rack over cookie sheet. In a small pan over low heat, stir chocolate chips and condensed milk and heat until chips are melted. Stir in cherry juice. Spoon 1 teaspoon chocolate over each cherry cookie, spreading to cover cherry. Let set until chocolate is firm.   Makes 4 dozen.

Gingerbread Men

3 1/4	cups all-purpose flour	3/4	cup firmly packed dark brown sugar
1/4	teaspoon salt		
1/2	teaspoon baking soda	1	large egg
1/4	teaspoon ground cloves	1/2	cup unsulphured molasses
2	teaspoons ground ginger	1/2	cup raisins
1	teaspoon ground cinnamon	2/3	cup confectioners' sugar
2	sticks butter, softened to room temperature	1 to 2	teaspoons milk

Whisk together first 6 ingredients. Set aside. In separate bowl, cream butter and sugar with a mixer. Add egg and molasses; beat on medium until mixture is smooth. Add the flour mixture. Blend on low just until mixture is combined. Divide dough in half and form into flat rounds. Cover each tightly with plastic wrap. Chill for 1 hour or until firm. Preheat oven to 325°. Flour rolling pin and board. Roll each half of dough out to form a 1/4-inch thickness. Flour cookie cutters; cut out gingerbread people. Continue to roll and cut out dough until all is used. Place 1/2 inch apart on ungreased cookie sheets. Soak raisins in warm water for 5 minutes and drain. Place raisins as eyes, noses, and mouths. Bake for 9 to 11 minutes. Do not brown. Use a spatula to place on flat surface to cool. Combine confectioners' sugar and milk in a small bowl. Stir until smooth. If too dry, add more milk a bit at a time. Place icing in a pastry bag with a small tip. Decorate.   Makes about 40 cookies.

Decorate your tree with gingerbread men! Before baking, punch a hole at the top with a straw, or at the hands to pull ribbon through and string them on your tree!

Christmas Eggnog Cookies

Try these cheery cookies on top of eggnog or vanilla ice cream...Yum!

2 1/4	cups all-purpose flour
1	teaspoon baking powder
1/2	teaspoon ground nutmeg
1/2	teaspoon ground cinnamon
1 1/2	sticks salted butter, softened to room temperature
1 1/4	cups sugar
1	teaspoon vanilla extract
2	large egg yolks
1/2	cup eggnog
	Ground nutmeg

Preheat oven to 300°. Combine flour, baking powder, nutmeg, and cinnamon, and set aside. In a separate bowl, use a mixer to cream butter and sugar. Add vanilla, egg yolks, and eggnog. Beat on medium until mixture is smooth. Add the flour mixture and beat on low just until mixture is combined. Drop by the teaspoon, 1 inch apart, onto ungreased cookie sheets. Sprinkle with nutmeg. Bake for 20 to 22 minutes or until bottoms turn light brown. Use a spatula to place cookies on wire rack to cool.

Makes 36 cookies.

Festive Peanut Kisses

3/4	cup peanut butter	1 1/2	cups unsifted all-purpose flour	
1/2	cup vegetable shortening			
1/3	cup sugar	1/2	teaspoon salt	
1/3	cup firmly packed brown sugar	1	teaspoon baking soda sugar	
1	egg	1	9-ounce package milk chocolate candy kisses	
2	tablespoons milk			
1	teaspoon vanilla extract			

Be Sure to share these "Peanut Kisses" under the mistletoe!

Preheat oven to 375°. Cream peanut butter and shortening together in large bowl. Blend in both sugars. Add egg, milk, and vanilla; beat well. In a separate bowl, combine flour, salt, and baking soda. Slowly add flour mixture to creamed mixture; blend thoroughly. Form dough into 1-inch balls. Roll in sugar. Place on an ungreased cookie sheet. Bake for 10 to 12 minutes. Remove from oven. Immediately place an unwrapped candy on top of each cookie. Press down until cookie cracks around the edges. Remove from cookie sheet. Use a spatula to place cookies on a wire rack to cool.

Makes about 48 cookies.

Merry Macaroons

"C" is for Cookie!

—The Cookie Monster from Sesame Street

1/3	cup butter or margarine, softened to room temperature	2	teaspoons strong coffee
		2	teaspoons almond extract
1	3-ounce package cream cheese, softened to room temperature	1 1/4	cups unsifted all-purpose flour
		2	teaspoons baking powder
3/4	cup sugar	1/4	teaspoon salt
1	egg yolk	1	14-ounce package flaked coconut, divided

Cream butter, cream cheese, and sugar together in a large bowl. Add egg yolk, coffee, and almond extract; blend well. In a separate bowl, combine flour, baking powder, and salt. Slowly add flour mixture to creamed mixture. Stir in 3 cups of the flaked coconut. Chill dough for 1 hour. Preheat oven to 350°. Form dough into 1-inch balls. Roll balls in remaining coconut. Place on an ungreased cookie sheet; flatten with a fork. Bake for 12 to 15 minutes or until lightly browned on the bottoms. Remove from oven. Carefully remove cookies with spatula and place on wire rack to cool.

Makes about 50 cookies.

Chocolate Orange Balls

1	12-ounce package vanilla wafers, crushed
3/4	cup confectioners' sugar
1/4	cup cocoa
1 1/2	cups chopped nuts
3	tablespoons light corn syrup
1/2	cup orange juice plus 1 teaspoon grated orange peel
	Confectioners' sugar

Combine crumbs, sugar, cocoa, and nuts in a large bowl. Blend in corn syrup, orange juice, and grated peel. Form into 1-inch balls. Roll in confectioners' sugar. Store in an airtight container several days to develop flavor. Roll again in confectioners' sugar before serving.

Makes about 48 cookies.

Crumble broken Christmas cookies, put into colorful plastic cups, and let your children sprinkle the cookies across the snow to feed the birds throughout the holiday season.

Black and White Christmas Cookies

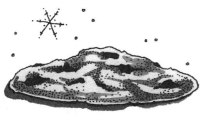

Fill your home with the scents of the holiday by simmering spices together such as cinnamon and vanilla!

2	sticks butter or margarine, softened to room temperature
1 1/2	cups sugar
2	eggs
2	teaspoons vanilla extract
2	cups unsifted all-purpose flour
2/3	cup cocoa
1/2	teaspoon salt
3/4	teaspoon baking soda
1	12-ounce package white chocolate chips

Cream butter, sugar, eggs, and vanilla in a large bowl. In a separate bowl, combine flour, cocoa, salt, and baking soda. Slowly add flour mixture to creamed mixture. Stir in chips. Chill until firm enough to handle. Preheat oven to 350°. Form into 1-inch balls. Place on an ungreased cookie sheet. Flatten slightly with a fork. Bake for 8 to 10 minutes. Cool for 1 minute on cookie sheet. Use a spatula to place cookies on wire rack to cool.

Makes about 60 cookies.

Lacy Oatmeal Cookies

1/4	cup all-purpose flour
1	cup quick-cooking oats
1 1/2	teaspoons baking powder
1/2	teaspoon salt
1	stick butter, softened to room temperature
1	cup sugar
1	large egg
1	teaspoon vanilla extract

Try serving these Lacy Oatmeal Christmas Cookies, on a lace table cloth, with red satin ribbons laced and tied along the hem!

Preheat oven to 325°. Line cookie sheets with foil. Spray lightly with nonstick vegetable spray. Combine flour, oats, baking powder, and salt, and set aside. In a separate bowl, use a mixer on medium to cream butter and sugar. Add egg and vanilla, and beat on medium until mixture is smooth. Add flour mixture and blend just until mixture is combined. Drop dough by the teaspoon, 2 1/2 inches apart, onto lined cookie sheets. Bake for 10 to 12 minutes or until the edges start to lightly brown. Cool on cookie sheets, then gently peel cookies with fingers.

Makes about 100 cookies.

Gingersnaps

Remember: It's never too late in the evening for warm cookies and milk!

3/4	cup vegetable shortening
1	cup sugar
1	egg
1/4	teaspoon salt
4	tablespoons molasses
2	cups all-purpose flour
3	teaspoons baking soda
1	teaspoon ginger
1	teaspoon cinnamon
1/2	teaspoon ground cloves

Preheat oven to 350°. In a large bowl, cream together the shortening and sugar, with mixer on medium, until light. Add the egg, salt, and molasses; mix well. In a separate bowl, sift together the next 5 ingredients. Slowly blend into the creamed mixture a little at a time. Form dough into small balls; roll in sugar. Place on a greased cookie sheet. Bake for 10 to 12 minutes or until lightly browned.

Makes about 60 cookies.

Buttery Cinnamon Cookies

3	tablespoons sugar		1	cup firmly packed dark brown sugar
1	tablespoon ground cinnamon			
2 1/2	cups all-purpose flour		2	sticks salted butter, softened to room temperature
1/4	teaspoon salt			
1/2	teaspoon baking soda		2	large eggs
1/2	cup sugar		2	teaspoons vanilla extract

Don't forget to leave a big, heaping platter of cookies for Santa!

Preheat oven to 300°. Combine 3 tablespoons sugar and cinnamon; set aside. In a medium bowl, combine flour, salt, and soda. Mix well and set aside. Blend sugars in a separate bowl. Add the butter using a mixer on medium. Add the eggs and vanilla. Blend on medium until mixture is light and fluffy. Add the flour mixture and mix on low just until mixture is combined. Form dough into 1-inch balls. Roll each ball in cinnamon-sugar. Place balls, 2 inches apart, onto ungreased cookie sheets. Bake for 18 to 20 minutes. Use a spatula to place cookies on wire rack to cool.

Makes 36 cookies.

Sugar Drops

2/3	cup vegetable shortening
1 2/3	cups sugar
2	eggs
2	teaspoons vanilla extract
3 1/2	cups sifted all-purpose flour
2	teaspoons baking powder
1	teaspoon salt
1/2	teaspoon baking soda
1/2	cup dairy sour cream

Preheat oven to 375°. In a large bowl, cream shortening and sugar, with mixer on medium, until smooth. Add eggs and vanilla; blend well. Stir together dry ingredients. Add dry ingredients, alternately with sour cream, to creamed mixture, beating well after each addition. Drop batter by the teaspoon, 2 inches apart, onto an ungreased cookie sheet. Bake for 10 to 12 minutes or until lightly golden. Use a spatula to place cookies on wire rack to cool.

Makes about 60 cookies.

No-Bake Fudge Cookies

1	cup sugar
1/2	cup whipping cream
1/2	stick butter, softened to room temperature
2	cups semisweet chocolate chips
1	teaspoon vanilla extract
2 1/2	cups quick-cooking oats
1	cup cherry preserves
1/4	cup confectioners' sugar

Surprise your children with cookies in their school lunch. Wrap them with plastic color wraps and ribbon to make them festive – and include a happy Christmas note!

Combine sugar, cream, and butter in a medium saucepan. Stir over medium heat until sugar is dissolved. Remove from heat. Add chocolate chips and vanilla. Stir until the chocolate melts and mixture is well combined. Add oats; stir until all ingredients are well blended. Form dough into 1-inch balls. Place on a wax paper-lined cookie sheet. Use the bottom of a glass to flatten cookies to about 2 inches each. Press thumb into center of each cookie. Chill cookies for one hour. Spoon 1/2 teaspoon of preserves into center of each cookie. Dust lightly with confectioners' sugar.

Makes about 30 cookies.

Ginger-Molasses Cookies

This Christmas, surprise your family one morning with warm cookies and cold milk for breakfast!

3/4	cup vegetable shortening
1	cup sugar
1	egg, beaten
2	teaspoons baking soda
4	tablespoons molasses
2	cups all-purpose flour
1	teaspoon ground ginger
1/2	teaspoon cinnamon
1/2	cup sugar

In a large bowl, cream shortening and sugar, with mixer on medium, until light. Blend in egg. Add baking soda to the molasses; stir until foamy. Fold into creamed mixture. Combine the next 3 ingredients and mix, a little at a time, into creamed mixture. Chill for 6 hours or overnight. Preheat oven to 325°. Form dough into 1-inch balls. Roll in sugar. Place on greased cookie sheet. Bake for 15 minutes or until golden. Use spatula to place cookies on wire rack to cool.

Makes 48 cookies.

Lemon Twists

1 1/3	sticks butter
3/4	cup sugar
1	egg, beaten
1 1/2	cups self-rising flour
1/4	cup ground almonds
1	teaspoon grated lemon rind

Next time carolers come-a-singing, have a platter of Christmas cookies ready to share with them!

Preheat oven to 400°. In a large bowl, cream butter and sugar, with mixer on medium, until light and fluffy. Stir in egg. Slowly add in flour, almonds, and lemon rind. Mix until well blended. Roll pieces of dough into 4-inch ropes. Twist into "S" shapes on greased cookie sheet. Bake for about 10 minutes or until golden. Use spatula to place cookies on wire rack to cool. Store in airtight container.

Makes about 48 cookies.

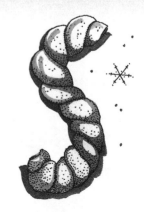

Snow-Capped Chocolate Cookies

Greet guests who come to your door throughout the holiday with a plate of homemade Christmas cookies!

1/2	cup vegetable shortening	2	cups sifted all-purpose flour
1 2/3	cups sugar	1/2	teaspoon salt
2	teaspoons vanilla extract	2	teaspoons baking powder
2	eggs	1/3	cup milk
2	1-ounce squares unsweetened chocolate, melted	1/2	cup chopped walnuts Confectioners' sugar

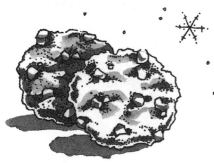

In a large bowl, cream shortening, sugar, and vanilla, with mixer on medium, until light. Beat in eggs. Stir in chocolate until well blended. Sift together dry ingredients. Blend into creamed mixture, alternately with milk. Stir in nuts. Chill for three hours. Form dough into 1-inch balls. Roll in confectioners' sugar. Place 2 to 3 inches apart on greased cookie sheet. Bake for 15 minutes. Cool slightly. Remove from pan. Dust with additional confectioners' sugar.

Makes about 48 cookies.

Chocolate Cashew Celebrations

2	sticks butter or margarine, softened to room temperature	1	teaspoon vanilla extract
		2 1/3	cups all-purpose flour
		2	teaspoons baking powder
2/3	cup sugar	1	teaspoon salt
1/2	cup chocolate syrup	1/4	cup milk
2	eggs		Cashews

In a large bowl, cream butter and sugar, with mixer on medium, until light and fluffy. Blend in chocolate syrup. Add eggs, one at a time, beating well after each addition. Blend in vanilla. Combine next 3 ingredients. Add flour mixture, alternately with milk, to chocolate mixture, beating well after each addition. Cover and chill for 1 hour. Preheat oven to 375°. Drop batter by the heaping teaspoon onto a greased cookie sheet. Press 4 cashews into each cookie. Bake for 10 to 12 minutes or until cookies spring back when lightly touched. Cool on cookie sheet for 2 minutes; use a spatula to place cookies on wire rack to cool completely.

Makes about 36 cookies.

Let your children join you in the kitchen. Even if just pressing in nuts or adding the final touch, it gives them a great sense of joy and satisfaction.

Chocolate Candy Cookies

Make a Family Christmas Cookie Cookbook in which you list the recipes of your favorite family cookie recipes. Add to it each year with new recipes.

2	tablespoons butter
1	8-ounce bar German chocolate
1/2	cup chopped pecans or walnuts
1	egg, beaten
1	cup confectioners' sugar
	Dash of salt
1	teaspoon vanilla extract
1	5-ounce package miniature marshmallows
	Coconut

Melt together the chocolate and butter. Stir in nuts and egg. Mix in remaining ingredients, except coconut. Chill mixture for 1 hour. Shape into a roll and cover with coconut. When ready to serve, slice into 1/4-inch slices.

Makes 60 cookies.

Grandma's Cookies

1	cup vegetable shortening
1	cup sugar
1	cup firmly packed brown sugar
2	eggs, beaten
2	cups all-purpose flour
2	cups crispy rice cereal
1	teaspoon baking soda
1/2	teaspoon salt
1	teaspoon vanilla extract
2	cups quick-cooking oats

If you don't have a Christmas-motif tablecloth, use a colorful quilt for a unique and welcoming touch on the table.

Preheat oven to 375°. In a large bowl, cream shortening and sugars, with mixer on medium, until light. Stir in eggs and flour. Blend in remaining ingredients. Form dough into small balls. Place on an ungreased cookie sheet. Press flat with the bottom of a glass dipped in sugar. Bake for 10 to 15 minutes or until lightly golden. Use spatula to place cookies on wire rack to cool.

Makes about 48 cookies.

Butterscotch Cookies

Make cookie lollipops by sticking popcicle sticks into your spooned-out dough, before placing the cookie sheet into the oven.

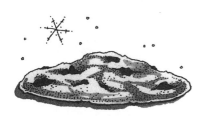

1 1/2	sticks butter or margarine, softened to room temperature
1/2	cup confectioners' sugar
1/4	teaspoon salt
1 3/4	cups all-purpose flour
1	12-ounce package butterscotch chips
3/4	cup chopped pecans

Preheat oven to 325°. In a large bowl, cream butter, sugar, and salt, with mixer on medium, until light and fluffy. Slowly add flour, a little at a time, beating until well blended. Stir in butterscotch chips and pecans. Drop dough by the teaspoon, 1 inch apart, onto a greased cookie sheet. Bake for 15 minutes or until cookies are set but not browned. Use a spatula to place cookies on wire rack to cool.

Makes 60 cookies.

Chewy Mocha Cookies

2	sticks butter, softened to room temperature	1/4	cup cocoa
1/2	cup sugar	1	cup finely chopped nuts
2	teaspoons vanilla extract	1/2	cup chopped maraschino cherries
2	cups sifted flour		Confectioners' sugar
1/2	teaspoon salt		
1	tablespoon powdered instant coffee		

Visit a shut-in — someone who can't get out much — and bring them a bunch of Christmas cookies!

In a large bowl, cream butter, with mixer on medium, until light and fluffy. Add sugar gradually; blend well. Stir in vanilla. Sift next 4 ingredients together; blend into creamed mixture, a little at a time. Stir in nuts and cherries. Cover and chill until dough can be handled easily. Preheat oven to 325°. Form dough into 1-inch balls. Place on greased cookie sheet. Bake for 20 minutes or until lightly browned. Dust warm cookies with confectioners' sugar.

Makes about 60 cookies.

Date Nut Dandies

Warm, homemade Christmas cookies make great Christmas memories!

2	eggs, beaten
1	cup sugar
1	stick butter
1	cup chopped dates
2 1/2	cups crispy rice cereal
1	cup chopped nuts
	Grated coconut

In saucepan, combine eggs, sugar, butter, and dates. Bring to a rapid boil. Boil for 4 minutes, stirring constantly. Remove from heat; stir in cereal and nuts. Form into small balls. Roll in coconut. Place on waxed paper.

Makes about 40 cookies.

Snowballs

4	sticks butter or margarine, melted
2	teaspoons vanilla extract
2	cups finely ground pecans
6	tablespoons confectioners' sugar
4	cups all-purpose flour
	Confectioners' sugar

Start making your Christmas cookies early in December before the pressure of the holiday sets in.

Preheat oven to 325°. Mix first 5 ingredients well. Form into 1-inch balls. Place on ungreased cookie sheet. Bake for 10 to 20 minutes until cookies turn lightly brown. Remove from oven; cool for 5 minutes. Roll each cookie in confectioners' sugar. When cool, roll again until well coated. If cookies break up while rolling in sugar, cool for another 5 minutes.

Makes about 100 cookies.

No-Bake Orange Buttons

Make lots of Christmas cookies at once. Make a weekend of it.

1	6-ounce can frozen orange juice concentrate, thawed
1	12 1/2-ounce box vanilla wafers, crushed
1	1-pound box confectioners' sugar
1	stick butter, softened to room temperature
	Shredded coconut

In large bowl, combine first 4 ingredients. Mix well. Form into small balls; roll in coconut.

Makes 80 cookies.

Icebox Cookies

4	sticks butter, softened to room temperature
1 1/2	cups sugar
1	1-pound box brown sugar
4	eggs
2	teaspoons vanilla extract
2	teaspoons cream of tartar
2	teaspoons baking soda
1	cup chopped pecans
7	cups flour
1	cup chopped dates

In a large bowl, cream butter and sugars together, with mixer on medium, until creamy. Mix in remaining ingredients until well blended. Form dough into rolls; wrap in plastic wrap. Chill overnight. Slice and bake as needed for 8 to 10 minutes in a 400° oven.

Makes about 100 cookies.

Hiding a box of cookies for a treasure hunt makes a fun game for children. It can be for a large Christmas party or just for fun at home! Place them in a neat tin with gold chocolate coins and other treats!

Soft Cinnamon-Sugar Marbles

Freeze your Christmas cookies in batches. Pull them out of the freezer as you need them throughout the holiday.

2 3/4	cups all-purpose flour
1	teaspoon baking soda
2	teaspoons cream of tartar
1/2	teaspoon salt
1	cup vegetable shortening
1 1/2	cups sugar
2	eggs
4	tablespoons sugar mixed with 4 teaspoons cinnamon

Mix first four ingredients; set aside. In a large bowl, cream shortening, sugar, and eggs, with a mixer on medium, until fluffy. On low speed, beat in flour mixture, a little at a time. Chill until dough is easy to handle. Preheat oven to 400°. Form into 1/2-inch balls. Roll in sugar/cinnamon mixture. Place on ungreased cookie sheet. Bake for 8 to 10 minutes or until lightly golden.

Makes about 48 cookies.

Butter-Nut Buttons

2	sticks butter, softened to room temperature
1/2	cup confectioners' sugar
1/2	teaspoon vanilla extract
1 3/4	cups all-purpose flour
1/2	cup chopped pecans

Pack the Christmas cookies you give to others in colorful, inexpensive tin boxes!

In a large bowl, cream butter and sugar, with mixer on medium, until light and fluffy. Blend in vanilla. Gradually add flour; blend well. Stir in nuts. Cover dough and chill until firm. Preheat oven to 350°. Form dough into 1-inch balls. Place on a greased baking sheet. Bake for 20 minutes or until golden brown. Use a spatula to place cookies on wire rack to cool.

Makes about 36 cookies.

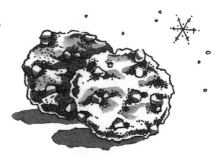

Chewy Cherry Surprise Cookies

Bake Christmas cookies which sparkle with a variety of colors, especially red, white, green, and gold.

1 1/2	cups all-purpose flour
1/4	cup sugar
1	stick butter, softened to room temperature
1	egg
1/4	teaspoon salt

1	teaspoon vanilla extract
1	teaspoon grated lemon peel
1/4	cup finely chopped nuts
1	16-ounce can cherry pie filling
	Confectioners' sugar

Preheat oven to 350°. In a large bowl, combine first 6 ingredients; blend well. Stir in lemon peel and nuts. Form dough into 1-inch balls. Place on an ungreased cookie sheet. Press thumb deeply into center of each ball. Bake for 10 minutes or until cookies are lightly browned. Use spatula to place cookies on wire rack to cool. Dust cookies with confectioners' sugar. Spoon one cherry with a small amount of filling into the center of each cookie. Fill cookies just before they are to be served. Sprinkle with additional confectioners' sugar, if desired.

Makes about 36 cookies.

Almond Cookies

2	sticks butter, softened to room temperature
3	tablespoons sugar
1	teaspoon almond extract
2	cups all-purpose flour
1/2	teaspoon salt
	sliced, unblanched almonds

In a large bowl, cream butter and sugar, with mixer on medium, until light and fluffy. Blend in almond extract. Combine flour and salt. Add flour mixture to creamed mixture, a little at a time, until well blended. Cover dough with plastic wrap and chill until firm. Preheat oven to 400°. Form dough into 3/4-inch balls. Place on an ungreased cookie sheet. Using the bottom of a glass dipped in sugar, flatten balls to 1/4-inch thickness. Top each with sliced almond. Bake for 5 to 6 minutes or just until golden. Use spatula to place cookies on wire rack to cool.

Makes about 60 cookies.

Make your cookie baking more enjoyable. Wear athletic shoes which support your arches and cushion against the hard floor.

Triple Almond Macaroons

Make baking fun! Reward yourself between batches of Christmas cookies by sticking your feet up and savoring a cup of hot cocoa or cinnamon tea with honey.

1 1/2	cups sugar
1/4	teaspoon salt
1	teaspoon almond extract
1 1/2	cups ground blanched almonds
3	egg whites
2	tablespoons all-purpose flour
	Blanched whole almonds

Preheat oven to 325°. In a large bowl, combine first four ingredients. Add egg whites; beat until stiff. Sprinkle flour over batter; fold in with a rubber spatula. Using a tablespoon, form dough into balls. Place on a greased and floured cookie sheet. Flatten balls slightly, using the back of a spoon. Place an almond in the center of each cookie. Bake for 20 minutes or until lightly browned. Use spatula to place cookies on wire rack to cool.

Makes about 30 cookies.

No-Bake Chocolate Peanut Butter Balls

1	12-ounce package peanut butter chips
1	stick butter
2	cups puffed rice cereal
1 1/2	cups confectioners' sugar
1	cup chopped pecans
1	12-ounce package milk chocolate chips
1/2	cup vegetable shortening

Be flexible! If the family interrupts your baking, give them your time. The kitchen will always be there later.

In a large saucepan, combine peanut butter chips and butter. Stir constantly over low heat until smooth. Remove from heat. Stir in cereal, sugar, and nuts. Form dough into 1-inch balls. Chill for 1 hour or more. In a small saucepan, combine milk chocolate chips and shortening. Stir constantly over low heat until smooth. Use a skewer or toothpick to dip balls into chocolate. Place on wax paper-lined cookie sheet. Chill before serving.

Makes about 30 cookies.

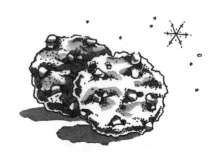

Vanilla Cookies

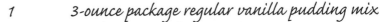

When serving your Christmas cookies, display each different batch of cookies on a different shape and color of plate!

1	3-ounce package regular vanilla pudding mix
1	cup buttermilk baking mix
1/4	cup vegetable shortening
2	tablespoons milk
1	egg, beaten

Preheat oven to 375°. In a large bowl, combine pudding and baking mix. Cut in shortening with a pastry blender or two knives until mixture resembles coarse crumbs. Stir in milk and egg until well blended. Form dough into small balls. Place on an ungreased cookie sheet. Flatten balls with the back of a spoon. Bake for 10 to 12 minutes or until golden brown. Use spatula to place cookies on wire rack to cool.

Makes 24 cookies.

Crispy Date Nut Balls

3/4	cup sugar
1	stick butter
2	8-ounce packages pitted dates, chopped
2	tablespoons milk
1	egg, slightly beaten
1	teaspoon salt
1	teaspoon vanilla extract
3/4	cup chopped nuts
2	cups crispy rice cereal
2	cups chocolate sprinkles

Make it easy on yourself! Bake your Christmas cookies on inexpensive, disposable aluminum pans. When done, throw them away and go play!

In a saucepan, combine sugar, butter, and dates. Bring to a boil. Stir constantly over medium heat until thickened. Add milk, egg, and salt; boil for 2 minutes. Remove from heat; cool. Blend in vanilla. Stir in nuts and cereal. Form dough into 1-inch balls. Roll in sprinkles.

Makes about 48 cookies.

Pecan Balls

Tickle the family palette! When choosing your Christmas cookie recipes, pick a variety of textures as well as flavors.

1	*stick butter*
1	*cup all-purpose flour*
2	*tablespoons sugar*
1	*teaspoon vanilla extract*
1/8	*teaspoon salt*
1	*cup chopped pecans*
	Confectioners' sugar

Preheat oven to 375°. In a large bowl, combine all ingredients, except confectioners' sugar; blend well. Form into 1-inch balls. Place on ungreased cookie sheet. Bake for 20 minutes. Remove from pan and roll each ball in confectioners' sugar.

Makes about 36 cookies.

Oatmeal Christmas Crispies

1	stick butter or margarine, softened to room temperature
1/2	cup sugar
1/2	cup firmly packed brown sugar
1	egg
1/2	teaspoon vanilla extract
3/4	cup all-purpose flour
1/2	teaspoon baking soda
1/2	teaspoon salt
1 1/2	cups quick-cooking oats
1/2	teaspoon ground cinnamon mixed with 1/4 cup sugar

Surprise your "Secret Pal" with cookies festively wrapped!

Preheat oven to 350°. In a large bowl, cream butter and sugars with mixer on medium. Add egg and vanilla and blend on high until mixture is white. Add next 3 ingredients, and mix until well blended. Stir in oats. Form into 1-inch balls; roll in cinnamon-sugar mixture. Bake for 8 to 10 minutes. Do not brown.

Makes 36 cookies.

Melting Moments

Bake a down-home Christmas! Bake cookies with oatmeal, raisins, shredded coconut, pecans, walnuts, cocoa, sugar, vanilla, cinnamon, and butter.

1	cup all-purpose flour
2	tablespoons cornstarch
1/2	cup confectioners' sugar
2	sticks butter, softened to room temperature
1 1/2	cups coconut

Preheat oven to 300°. In a large bowl, combine flour, cornstarch, and sugar. Cream in butter, with mixer on medium, until soft dough forms. Form into 3/4-inch balls. Roll in coconut. Place 1 1/2 inches apart on ungreased cookie sheet. Bake for 20 to 25 minutes, or until lightly browned.

Makes about 30 cookies.

Holiday Honey-Nut Cookies

2	sticks butter, softened to room temperature
1/4	cup honey
2	teaspoons vanilla extract
2	cups all-purpose flour
2	cups chopped walnuts
1/2	teaspoon salt

In a large bowl, cream butter, with mixer on high, until light. Beat in honey and vanilla until well blended. Beat in flour, walnuts, and salt until dough forms. Cover with plastic wrap and chill for 2 hours. Preheat oven to 325°. Flour hands and form dough into 1-inch balls. Place balls, about 2 inches apart on ungreased large cookie sheet. Use a fork to press balls down in crisscross pattern. Bake for 18 to 22 minutes or until golden. Use spatula to place cookies on wire rack to cool.

Makes about 36 cookies.

Make baking Christmas cookies a family day! Rotate duties: one prepares the raw dough, one forms them on the pan, one pulls them out of the oven, cools, and lifts them onto the plate, one cleans up.

Iced Almond Cookies

Tie colorful Christmas ribbon into a bow and place on the edge of the cookie platter.

2 1/2	cups all-purpose flour	1	teaspoon vanilla extract
1	tablespoon baking powder	3/4	cup confectioners' sugar
1	stick butter, softened to room temperature	2	tablespoons water
1/2	cup sugar		Red and green decorating sugar
3	large eggs		
2	teaspoons almond extract, divided		

Combine flour and baking powder; set aside. In a large bowl, cream butter and sugar, with mixer on medium, until creamy. Beat in eggs, 1 teaspoon almond extract, and vanilla. Reduce speed to low; beat in flour mixture, a little at a time, until well blended. Form dough into 4 equal parts. Wrap each in plastic wrap. Freeze for 1 hour or chill overnight. Preheat oven to 350°. On a lightly floured surface, divide 1 part of dough into 9 equal pieces, keeping remaining dough chilled. Flour hands and roll each piece of dough to form a 7-inch rope; bring ends together and lightly twist together. Pinch ends to seal. Place cookies, about 2 inches apart, on ungreased cookie sheet. Bake cookies for 12 minutes or until bottoms are lightly brown. Use spatula to place cookies on wire rack to cool. While cookies are cooling, combine confectioners' sugar with remaining teaspoon almond extract and water. Spread over tops of cookies. Sprinkle with decorating sugar.   Makes 36 cookies.

Iced Spice Cookies

2	sticks butter, softened to room temperature	1/4	teaspoon ground cloves
2 1/2	cups sugar, divided	2	teaspoons ground ginger
5 1/2	cups all-purpose flour	1/2	teaspoon ground nutmeg
1	cup light molasses	1	envelope unflavored gelatin
1/2	cup strong cold coffee	1	cup cold water
1/2	teaspoon salt	2	cups confectioners' sugar
2	teaspoons baking soda	1/4	teaspoon vanilla extract

Sprinkle red hots or green and red sparkles around the edge of the platter on which you serve your Christmas cookies.

In large bowl, cream butter and 1 1/2 cups sugar, with mixer on medium, until creamy. Add flour, molasses, and coffee. Add next 5 ingredients. Beat until mixture is well blended. Cover with plastic wrap. Chill for 2 hours or until dough is firm enough to handle. Divide dough into 3 equal parts. Form each part into a 12-inch log. Wrap each in plastic wrap. Freeze for 4 hours or overnight, until dough is firm enough to slice. Preheat oven to 350°. Slice each log into 1/4-inch thick slices. Place slices, 1 1/2 inches apart on greased cookie sheets. Bake 15 to 20 minutes or until lightly browned around the edges. Cool on cookie sheet 1 minute; use spatula to place cookies on a wire rack to cool completely. While cookies are cooling, combine remaining 1 cup sugar and gelatin in a saucepan; stir until well mixed. Add cold water; heat to boiling. Reduce heat to low and simmer, uncovered, for 10 minutes. In a separate bowl, combine confectioners' sugar and gelatin mixture, with mixer on low, until blended. Beat on high until fluffy. Beat in vanilla. Ice cookies. Set cookies aside for 1 hour to dry icing completely.   Makes about 100 cookies.

Dandy Dunkin' Sticks

Add at least one Old-World Christmas cookie recipe to your baking each year. Best yet, choose cookies which reflect your family heritage.

2	sticks butter, softened to room temperature (no substitute)
1/2	cup confectioners' sugar
1	teaspoon vanilla extract
2	cups all-purpose flour
1/2	cup mini semisweet chocolate chips

Cream butter, sugar, and vanilla, with mixer on medium, until light and fluffy. Reduce speed to low. Beat in flour, a little at a time, just until blended. Stir in chocolate chips. Divide dough into 2 parts and flatten slightly. Cover with plastic wrap; chill for 4 hours. Preheat oven to 350°. With floured hands, roll rounded teaspoons of dough to form 2 1/2-inch-long sticks. Place, 2 inches apart, on greased cookie sheets. Place in freezer for 10 minutes. Bake for 12 minutes or until edges are golden. Cool cookies on pans for 2 minutes, then use spatula to place cookies on wire racks to cool completely.

Makes 48 cookies.

Merry Melt In Your Mouth Cookies

1	cup macadamia nuts
1/2	cup confectioners' sugar, divided
2	sticks unsalted butter or margarine, softened to room temperature
1	teaspoon vanilla extract
2 1/2	cups all-purpose flour
	sifted confectioners' sugar

For fun, select a Christmas cookie theme: Christmas Cookies from England, France, Italy, or Spain.

Preheat oven to 350°. Rub nuts with a paper towel to remove salt. Finely grind nuts with 1/4 cup sugar. Set aside. Cream remaining 1/4 cup sugar, butter, and vanilla, with mixer on medium, until creamy. Reduce speed to low. Beat in flour, a little at a time, until blended. Stir in nut mixture. Shape dough into a ball. With floured hands, form dough into 1-inch balls. Place, 1 inch apart, on ungreased cookie sheets. Bake for 12 to 15 minutes until bottoms are lightly browned. Use spatula to place cookies on wire racks. While still warm, roll cookies in confectioners' sugar. Cool completely. Before serving, roll cookies in more sugar.

Makes 48 cookies.

Cream Cheese Pinwheels

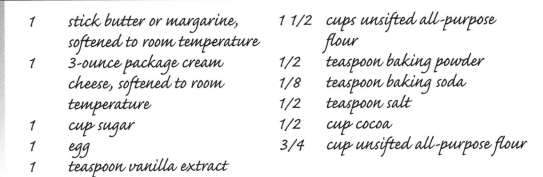

While cleaning up after your Christmas cookie baking, wear rubber gloves to save your nails for those holiday parties.

1	stick butter or margarine, softened to room temperature	1 1/2	cups unsifted all-purpose flour
1	3-ounce package cream cheese, softened to room temperature	1/2	teaspoon baking powder
		1/8	teaspoon baking soda
1	cup sugar	1/2	teaspoon salt
1	egg	1/2	cup cocoa
1	teaspoon vanilla extract	3/4	cup unsifted all-purpose flour

Cream butter, cream cheese, sugar, egg, and vanilla in a large bowl. In a separate bowl, combine 1 1/2 cups flour, baking powder, baking soda, and salt. Slowly add flour mixture to creamed mixture; blend well. Divide dough into equal parts. Blend cocoa into one part of the dough. Blend 3/4 cup flour into remaining dough. Form each part into a 9-inch square. (If dough is too soft, chill for 15 minutes.) Place plain layer on top of chocolate layer; roll up jelly-roll style. Cover and wrap tightly in plastic wrap. Chill for at least 1 hour or overnight. Preheat oven to 350°. Cut dough into 1/4-inch thick slices. Place on an ungreased cookie sheet. Bake for 12 to 15 minutes or until lightly browned. Use a spatula to place cookies on a wire rack to cool.   Makes about 36 cookies.

Christmas Ornament Cookies

1	stick butter or margarine, softened to room temperature	1 1/2	cups unsifted all-purpose flour
3/4	cup sugar	1/3	cup cocoa
1	egg	1/8	teaspoon salt
3/4	teaspoon peppermint extract	1/2	teaspoon baking powder
1	tablespoon milk		Red-hot candies, sprinkles, or gumdrops

Cream butter, sugar, egg, extract, and milk in a large bowl until light and fluffy. In a separate bowl, combine flour, cocoa, salt, and baking powder. Stir to blend. Slowly add flour mixture to creamed mixture; blend well. Divide dough into fourths. Cover and wrap tightly in plastic wrap; chill 2 to 3 hours. Preheat oven to 325°. Roll out dough, one fourth at a time, to a 1/8-inch thickness on a lightly floured board. Cut out the dough with Christmas-shaped cookie cutters. With a skewer, make a hole in the top of each cookie for hanging on the tree. Place cookies, 1 inch apart, on an ungreased cookie sheet. Use candies, sprinkles or gumdrops to decorate tops of cookies. Bake for 8 to 10 minutes or until firm. Use a spatula to place cookies on a wire rack to cool.

Makes about 24 cookies.

Invite friends and family over for a tree trimming party. Serve your cookies with hot cider. But, save some of your cookies for the tree!

Fruitcake Cookies

For a special touch, use festive holiday pot-holders, wash cloths, and kitchen towels when baking your Christmas cookies.

2	cups all-purpose flour	2	teaspoons vanilla extract
1/2	teaspoon baking powder	2	teaspoons almond extract
1	cup quick-cooking oats	2	large eggs
2	sticks butter, softened to room temperature	2	cups chopped candied cherries
1 1/2	cups firmly packed light brown sugar	1/2	cup raisins
1/4	cup unsulphured molasses	1/2	cup chopped almonds
2	teaspoons strong coffee	1	cup chopped pecans
			Candied cherries, halved

Preheat oven to 300°. Combine flour, baking powder, and oats, and set aside. In a separate bowl, use a mixer on medium to cream butter and sugar. Beat in molasses, coffee, extracts, and eggs until mixture is smooth. Add the flour mixture and remaining ingredients, except cherry halves. Mix on low just until mixture is blended. Drop by the tablespoon, 1 1/2 inches apart, onto ungreased cookie sheets. Bake for 20 to 25 minutes or until cookies are set. Cool cookies on pan for 5 minutes, then use a spatula to place on a wire rack to cool completely. Place a candied cherry half on each cookie.

Makes about 48 cookies.

Light as Air Chocolate Meringues

3/4	cup sifted confectioners' sugar
3	tablespoons sifted unsweetened cocoa
3	large egg whites
1/2	teaspoon cream of tartar
1/2	cup sugar
2	ounces unsweetened baking chocolate, grated

Combine confectioners' sugar and cocoa and set aside. In a separate bowl, beat egg whites and cream of tartar, with a mixer on medium, until thickened. Raise speed to high. Add sugar slowly, a little at a time. Beat until mixture forms glossy, stiff peaks. Use a rubber spatula to slowly fold in cocoa mixture and grated chocolate. Fold just until mixture is blended. Spoon into a pastry bag fitted with a large star tip. Pipe meringue into desired shapes on foil-lined cookie sheets. Allow to dry at room temperature for about 1 hour or until no longer sticky to the touch. Preheat oven to 200°. Bake for 1 hour. Allow to cool completely.

Makes about 30 cookies.

Crescent Meltaways

To make your cookies unique, use the symbols of Christmas in your baking, such as stars, candy canes, trees, bells, sparkling lights, and the Cross.

2	sticks butter, softened to room temperature
3/4	cup sugar
1 1/2	teaspoons vanilla extract
2 1/2	cups all-purpose flour
1	cup finely chopped walnuts
1 1/2	ounces semisweet baking chocolate
1 1/2	teaspoons light corn syrup
1 1/2	teaspoons cream
	Chocolate sprinkles or flaked coconut

Preheat oven to 350°. In a large bowl, cream butter and sugar, with mixer on medium, until smooth. Add vanilla; blend well. Slowly blend in flour, a little at a time. Stir in nuts. Pinch off dough and form into rolls about 3 inches long. Place rolls on an ungreased baking sheet. Curve ends to form crescent shapes. Bake for 15 minutes or until golden. Cool slightly on pan. Use a spatula to place cookies on wire rack to cool completely. In a small saucepan, combine remaining ingredients, except sprinkles or coconut. Stir over low heat until smooth. Dip ends in glaze, then in sprinkles or coconut.

Makes about 60 cookies.

Pecan Chocolate Tarts

1	stick butter or margarine, softened to room temperature	3	tablespoons cornstarch	
2	3-ounce packages cream cheese, softened to room temperature	1	stick butter or margarine, melted	
1/2	cup vegetable shortening	2	tablespoons light corn syrup	
2	cups all-purpose flour	1	teaspoon vanilla extract	
2	eggs	1/2	cup finely chopped pecans	
3/4	cup sugar	3/4	cup mini semisweet chocolate chips	

In a large bowl, cream softened butter, cream cheese, and shortening until smooth. Gradually add flour, a little at a time, until well blended. Cover dough with plastic wrap; chill until firm. Form dough into 1-inch balls. Place balls in ungreased miniature muffin cups. Press dough firmly on bottom and up sides of muffin cups; set aside. Preheat oven to 350°. Combine eggs, sugar, and cornstarch; mix well. Blend in melted butter, corn syrup, and vanilla. Stir in pecans and chocolate chips. Spoon a heaping teaspoon of mixture into each shell. Bake for 20 to 25 minutes or until tarts are golden brown. Let cool in pan placed on a wire rack.   Makes about 48 tarts.

On the side of the Christmas cookie platter, keep a small stack of cocktail-size Christmas napkins both for presentation and to catch all those crumbs before they fall.

Christmas Curls

Keep spiced cinammon apple cider on hand to warm and serve alongside your Christmas cookies.

1	stick butter, softened to room temperature
1/2	cup sugar
1	teaspoon vanilla extract
2	egg whites
2/3	cup all-purpose flour

Preheat oven to 375°. In a large bowl, cream butter, sugar, and vanilla, with mixer on medium, until light and fluffy. Add egg whites and flour; blend well. Drop batter by the teaspoon, 3 inches apart, onto an ungreased cookie sheet. With the back of a spoon, spread each cookie out to form 3-inch rounds. Bake for 5 minutes or until edges are light brown. Working with 1 cookie at a time, loosen from cookie sheet with a spatula and then quickly wrap tightly around a wooden spoon. Slide cookie off spoon and place each, seam side-down, on a wire rack to cool.

Makes about 36 cookies.

Heavenly Pinwheels

3/4	cup vegetable shortening	1	teaspoon salt
1	cup sugar	1	teaspoon baking powder
2	eggs, beaten	2	1-ounce squares unsweetened
1	teaspoon vanilla extract		baking chocolate, melted and
2 1/2	cups all-purpose flour		cooled

In a large bowl, cream shortening and sugar, with mixer on medium, until smooth. Blend in eggs and vanilla. Combine flour, salt, and baking powder. Gradually add dry ingredients, a little at a time, to creamed mixture until well blended. Divide dough into 2 parts. Blend melted chocolate into one part. Cover with plastic wrap and chill both parts of dough until firm. Roll each half out to form a 12 x 9-inch rectangle. Place chocolate dough on top of plain dough. Roll dough out to about 1/4 inch thickness. Roll up from the long side. Wrap in plastic wrap and chill until firm. Preheat oven to 400°. Cut in 1/8-inch slices. Place on an ungreased cookie sheet. Bake for 8 to 10 minutes or until set. Use spatula to place cookies on wire rack to cool.

Makes 60 to 70 cookies.

Designate a cozy corner in your living area to place a small table with a Christmas candle, a space for your cookie platter, and a small Christmas book.

Chocolate Cherry Delights

Periodically, throughout the holiday season, wrap a large Christmas cookie in pretty tissue with a bow and leave on your children's pillows to find upon going to bed. Do the same for house guests.

2	sticks butter, softened to room temperature	1 1/2	teaspoons baking powder
1 1/2	cups sugar	1/2	cup diced candied cherries
1	egg, beaten	1	1-ounce square unsweetened baking chocolate, melted and cooled
2	teaspoons vanilla extract		Hot milk
2 1/2	cups all-purpose flour		
3/4	teaspoon salt		

In a large bowl, cream butter and sugar, with mixer on medium, until smooth. Add egg and vanilla; blend well. Combine flour, baking powder, and salt. Gradually add dry ingredients, a little at a time, to creamed mixture until well blended. Divide dough into 3 equal parts. Stir cherries into 1/3 of the dough. Blend chocolate evenly into 2 remaining parts. Form cherry dough into a 9 x 3/4-inch bar. Form both parts of chocolate dough into one 9 x 1 1/2-inch bar. Wrap each bar in plastic wrap and chill until firm. Cut chocolate dough in half lengthwise. Brush cut sides of chocolate dough with hot milk. Brush both sides of cherry dough with milk. Place cherry dough between the chocolate portions; press together. Wrap in plastic wrap and chill until firm. Preheat oven to 350°. Cut dough into 1/4-inch slices. Place on an ungreased cookie sheet. Bake for about 8 to 10 minutes or until set. Use spatula to place cookies on wire rack to cool.   Makes about 100 cookies.

Linzer Cookies

2	cups all-purpose flour		2	egg yolks, lightly beaten
1/2	cup confectioners' sugar		1/4	teaspoon cinnamon
1/4	teaspoon baking soda		1/2	teaspoon vanilla extract
1/4	cup finely ground almonds		1	egg, lightly beaten
1/4	cup sugar		1/2	cup raspberry jam
1	stick butter, chilled and cut into 1-inch pieces			Confectioners' sugar

Preheat oven to 350°. In a large bowl, combine first 3 ingredients. Stir in almonds and sugar. Cut in butter with a pastry blender or two knives until mixture resembles coarse crumbs. Stir in egg yolks, cinnamon, and vanilla until well blended. Shape dough into a ball. Turn out onto a lightly floured surface. Knead lightly; form into a smooth ball. Roll dough out between sheets of waxed paper to 1/4-inch thickness. Cut out with a floured 1 1/2-inch round cookie cutter. Use a thimble or donut hole cutter to cut holes in centers of half of the cookies. Brush all the cookies with beaten egg. Place on a large greased cookie sheet. Bake for 18 to 20 minutes or until golden brown. Use spatula to place cookies on wire rack to cool. Spread jam on whole cookies. Top each whole cookie with a cut-out cookie. Sprinkle with confectioners' sugar.   Makes about 24 cookies.

Glistening Glass Window Cookies

3	tablespoons butter, softened to room temperature	1/4	teaspoon nutmeg
		1/4	teaspoon ginger
1/2	cup firmly packed dark brown sugar	3	cups all-purpose flour
		1	teaspoon baking soda
3/4	cup molasses	1/2	teaspoon salt
1/3	cup water	1	5 3/4-ounce bag sourball candies
1/4	teaspoon cinnamon		

In a large bowl, cream together butter, brown sugar, and molasses until smooth. Blend in water. Combine next 6 ingredients. Gradually add flour mixture, a little at a time, to creamed mixture until well blended. Cover and chill for 1 hour. Preheat oven to 350°. Trace Christmas shapes onto a sheet of aluminum foil with a knife or dull pencil. Place foil on cookie sheets. Roll pieces of dough into ropes about 1/4-inch wide. Outline the foil shapes with ropes of dough. Press ends lightly together. Separate candies by color. Coarsely crush candies in a blender or food processor. Fill in dough outlines with the candies. Bake for 4 to 5 minutes or until cookies are set and candy is melted. Cool on cookie sheet.   Makes about 36 cookies.

Poinsettia Cookies

2	sticks butter or margarine, softened to room temperature	1	teaspoon salt
2	cups confectioners' sugar	1	cup shredded coconut
2	eggs	1	cup butterscotch-flavored chips, divided
1	teaspoon vanilla extract		Sugar
1/2	teaspoon rum extract	1/2	cup candied red cherries, cut into fourths
3	cups all-purpose flour		

In a large bowl, cream butter and sugar, with mixer on medium, until smooth. Blend in eggs and extracts. Combine flour and salt. Gradually add dry ingredients, a little at a time, to creamed mixture until well blended. Stir in coconut and 3/4 cup butterscotch chips. Chill dough until firm. Preheat oven to 375°. Form dough into 1-inch balls. Place on an ungreased cookie sheet. Flatten balls with the bottom of a glass dipped in sugar. Press a butterscotch chip in the center of each cookie. Arrange cherry pieces in a circle around chips. Bake for 10 to 12 minutes or until lightly golden. Use spatula to place cookies on wire rack to cool.

Makes about 60 cookies.

Christmas Candy Canes

Use as many fresh ingredients as you can when baking for best flavor and most nutritious content.

1/2	cup vegetable shortening	1	teaspoon almond extract
1	stick butter, softened to room temperature	1	teaspoon salt
2 1/2	cups all-purpose flour	1/2	teaspoon red food coloring
1	cup confectioners' sugar	1/2	cup finely crushed peppermint candy
1	egg, slightly beaten	1/2	cup sugar
1	teaspoon vanilla extract		

Preheat oven to 350°. In a large bowl, combine first 8 ingredients and mix until well blended. Divide dough into 2 equal parts; add red coloring to one part, blend until thoroughly mixed and color is even. Roll pieces of each dough to form 4-inch ropes. Place 1 rope of each color side by side; gently twist together. Curve one end down to form candy cane. Continue until all dough is used. Place candy canes on ungreased cookie sheets. Bake for 8 to 10 minutes, just until edges begin to brown. Combine crushed candy and 1/2 cup sugar; mix well. While still warm, carefully remove cookies from cookie sheets. Press or roll with candy mixture.

Makes about 48 cookies.

Fancy Fruit Cookies

1 1/2	sticks butter or margarine, softened to room temperature	2 1/2	cups all-purpose flour
1	cup sugar	1	teaspoon salt
2	eggs	1	teaspoon baking powder
1/2	teaspoon lemon extract	6	packages Fancy Fruit flavor Life-Savers

Cream butter, sugar, eggs, and extract. Blend in flour, salt, and baking powder. Cover; chill for 1 hour. Preheat oven to 375°. On a lightly floured cloth-covered surface, roll dough out to a 1/8-inch-thickness. Cut into fruit shapes, using cookie cutters of two sizes to make small and large cutouts, or create your own designs. Place cookies on a foil-covered cookie sheet. Place whole candies in the cutout. Break Life-Savers into pieces if needed to fit into shapes. Fill cuts until candy is just level with dough. Bake for 7 to 9 minutes or until cookies are lightly brown and candy is melted. If candy does not spread evenly, spread with a spatula. Cool completely on cookie sheet. Use spatula to remove cookies.

Makes 60 cookies.

Before baking, clear your countertops and organize all your cookie-baking ingredients and utensils to make your baking easier.

Holiday Hazelnut Cups

Keep in mind that the fewer ingredients a recipe has, the cheaper and easier it will be to prepare.

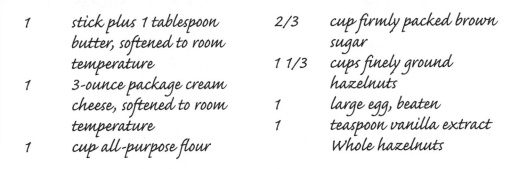

1	stick plus 1 tablespoon butter, softened to room temperature	2/3	cup firmly packed brown sugar
1	3-ounce package cream cheese, softened to room temperature	1 1/3	cups finely ground hazelnuts
1	cup all-purpose flour	1	large egg, beaten
		1	teaspoon vanilla extract
			Whole hazelnuts

In large bowl, cream 1 stick butter and cheese, with mixer on high, until light. Mix in flour until well blended. Cover with plastic wrap; chill for 30 minutes. Preheat oven to 350°. Mix brown sugar and nuts. In a separate bowl, combine sugar-nut mixture with egg, vanilla, and remaining butter. Flour hands and separate dough into 24 equal pieces. Gently press dough pieces onto bottom and sides of 24 ungreased miniature muffin cups. Spoon nut filling into each cup; place 1 hazelnut on top of each filled cup. Bake for 30 minutes or until filling is set and crust is golden. Use a knife to loosen cookies from muffin cups. Place on wire rack to cool completely.

Makes 24 cookies.

Biscotti

4	cups all-purpose flour, divided	1/2	cup vegetable shortening
1/2	teaspoon baking soda	1 1/2	cups sugar, divided
2	teaspoons baking powder	3	large eggs
1	stick butter, softened to room temperature	1	teaspoon vanilla extract
		1 1/2	teaspoons ground cinnamon

Combine 3 cups flour, baking soda, and baking powder; set aside. In a large bowl, cream butter, shortening, and 1 cup sugar, with mixer on medium, until light and fluffy. Beat in eggs, one at a time, then vanilla until well mixed. Add flour mixture, a little at a time, until well blended. Stir in remaining flour until a soft dough forms. Add up to 1/2 cup flour until dough is easy to handle. Preheat oven to 350°. Divide dough into 4 equal pieces and form each piece of dough into an 8-inch-long log. Place 2 logs each, about 4 inches apart, on 2 ungreased cookie sheets. Use a spatula to press each log to about 2 1/2 inches wide. Place cookie sheets on separate oven racks. Switch cookie sheets between racks after 10 minutes of baking. Bake for a total of 20 minutes or until lightly browned and toothpick inserted in center comes out clean. Combine cinnamon with remaining 1/2 cup sugar. Remove cookies from oven. Transfer cookies to cutting board. Cut diagonally into 1/2-inch-thick slices. Coat each slice with cinnamon sugar. Place slices, cut-side down, onto cookie sheets. Bake for 15 minutes. Turn slices over, and switch cookie sheets between racks. Bake for 15 minutes more or until golden. Place cookies onto wire racks to cool.   Makes about 48 cookies.

Get ready for the market by listing your cooking ingredients all on one list before going to the store.

Strawberry Stack Cookies

2 1/2 cups all-purpose flour, sifted
2 sticks butter, softened to room temperature and cut up (no substitute)
1 cup confectioners' sugar, sifted
1/2 cup finely ground blanched almonds
1 large egg yolk, beaten
1/2 teaspoon grated lemon peel
3/4 cup strawberry jam or preserves
Confectioners' sugar

Combine first 6 ingredients in a large bowl. Use hands to blend and lightly knead dough until it holds together. Divide dough into 4 equal parts and flatten slightly. Cover with plastic wrap and chill for 4 hours or until firm.

Preheat oven to 350°. Roll dough out on a lightly floured surface to a 1/8-inch thickness. Cut out equal number of circles with 2-inch, 1 1/2-inch, and 1-inch round cookie cutters. Place on greased cookie sheets. Bake for 6 to 10 minutes or until firm and edges are lightly golden. Use spatula to place cookies on wire racks to cool. When cool, place 1/4 teaspoon jam onto center of each 2-inch cookie. Press 1 1/2-inch cookies on top of jam. Place 1/8 teaspoon jam on top of 1 1/2-inch cookies. Top with 1-inch cookies. Press together lightly. Sprinkle with confectioners' sugar.   Makes 48 cookies.

Christmas In The Caribbean

5	tablespoons butter, softened to room temperature	1	cup well-drained, crushed pineapple
1/3	cup confectioners' sugar	1/2	cup firmly packed brown sugar
3/4	cup all-purpose flour		
1/4	teaspoon baking powder	1/4	cup chopped walnuts
1/4	teaspoon salt	1/4	cup flaked coconut
1/4	teaspoon almond extract	1	egg
1/8	teaspoon nutmeg	1	tablespoon all-purpose flour

Use as many natural ingredients as you can to keep Christmas cookies both fun and full of good health for your family.

Preheat oven to 350°. In a small bowl, cream butter and confectioners' sugar, with mixer on medium, until smooth. Add 3/4 cup flour; mix until crumbly. Press crumb mixture into an ungreased 8-inch square baking pan. Bake for 15 minutes or until light golden brown. Combine remaining ingredients; blend well. Spread over baked crust. Bake for 25 minutes or until golden brown. Cool in pan before cutting into squares.

Makes 16 cookies.

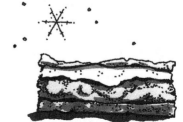

Strawberry Crisps

1 1/2	*sticks butter, softened to room temperature*
1	*cup firmly packed light brown sugar*
1 3/4	*cups all-purpose flour*
1/2	*teaspoon salt*
1/2	*teaspoon baking soda*
1 1/2	*cups quick-cooking rolled oats*
1	*18-ounce jar strawberry jam*

Preheat oven to 400°. In a large bowl, cream margarine and brown sugar, with mixer on medium, until smooth. Stir together dry ingredients. Gradually add dry ingredients to creamed mixture; mix until crumbly. Press 1/2 the mixture into a greased 13 x 9-inch baking pan. Spread with jam. Sprinkle remaining crumb mixture over the top; press lightly into jam. Bake for 18 to 20 minutes or until lightly browned. Cool for 5 minutes before cutting into squares.

Makes 24 cookies.

Chewy Chocolate-Walnut Cookies

1/2	stick butter, softened to room temperature	1	teaspoon vanilla extract
1	cup sifted all-purpose flour	1/4	teaspoon salt
1/4	teaspoon salt	2	tablespoons all-purpose flour
3/4	cup firmly packed light brown sugar	1	6-ounce package semisweet chocolate chips
2	eggs, slightly beaten	1 1/4	cups light corn syrup
1	cup chopped walnuts	1	tablespoon water
			Chopped pecans

Serve fresh fruits alongside your cookies to balance the sweet with nutrition.

Preheat oven to 350°. In a large bowl, combine butter, 1 cup flour, and salt with pastry blender; mix until crumbly. Press crumb mixture into a greased and floured 9-inch square baking pan. Bake for 15 minutes. In a small bowl, beat sugar and eggs until smooth. Stir in 1 cup nuts, vanilla, salt, and 2 tablespoons flour; blend well. Spread mixture over baked crust. Bake for 15 minutes; let cool. Melt chocolate chips in microwave. Blend in corn syrup and water. Spread chocolate mixture evenly over cooled cookies. Sprinkle with nuts. Set aside overnight. Cut into squares before serving.

Makes 24 cookies.

Chocolate Praline Cookies

Cull out your old Christmas cookie recipes you have tried and don't like, which look too difficult to make, which look too expensive to make; keep the ones you want to try!

1	stick plus 3 tablespoons butter
2	cups firmly packed brown sugar
2	eggs
1	teaspoon vanilla extract
1 1/2	cups all-purpose flour
1/4	teaspoon salt
2	teaspoons baking powder
1/2	cup chopped nuts
1	12-ounce package semisweet chocolate chips

Preheat oven to 350°. In a large saucepan, melt butter. Remove from heat and stir in sugar, eggs, and vanilla. Blend in the next 3 ingredients. Add nuts and chocolate chips. Place in greased 11 x 9-inch pan. Bake for 35 minutes. When cool, cut into squares.

Makes about 18 cookies.

Iced Butterscotch Chocolate Chip Bars

3/4	cup all-purpose flour	1	teaspoon vanilla extract
1/2	teaspoon salt	2 1/2	cups semisweet chocolate
1/2	teaspoon baking powder		chips, divided
1	stick butter or margarine	1/2	cup chopped walnuts
1	cup firmly packed dark		Butterscotch Icing (recipe
	brown sugar		follows)
2	eggs		

Preheat oven to 350°. Combine first 3 ingredients; set aside. Melt butter in a medium saucepan. Stir in brown sugar; heat on low until sugar melts. Add eggs, one at a time, beating well after each addition. Blend in vanilla. Add dry ingredients; blend well. Stir in 2 cups chocolate chips and nuts. Spread batter in a greased 8-inch square baking pan. Bake for 30 minutes or until set. Cool in pan. Prepare Butterscotch Frosting. Spread over cookies. Dot with remaining 1/2 cup chocolate chips. Cut into bars.

Makes 24 bars.

Butterscotch Icing

Develop a Christmas cookie "Speciality!" Make it a tradition which your family will remember for years to come.

1/2	stick butter or margarine, softened to room temperature
1/2	cup firmly packed dark brown sugar
1	tablespoon half-and-half
1/4	teaspoon vanilla extract

Cream butter and sugar, with mixer on medium, until smooth. Blend in half-and-half and vanilla. If frosting is too soft, chill for 10 minutes.

Crunchy Chewies

1 3/4	cups firmly packed brown sugar, divided
2	cups all-purpose flour
3	sticks butter, softened to room temperature, divided (no substitute)
1	cup chopped pecans
1	12-ounce package semisweet chocolate chips

Preheat oven to 350°. Cream 1 stick butter, 1 cup brown sugar, and flour. Press into an ungreased 9 x 13-inch pan. Sprinkle pecans evenly over top. Melt 2 sticks butter and remaining brown sugar in saucepan. Bring to a boil and boil for 1 minute, stirring constantly. Pour mixture over pecan-topped crust. Bake for 20 to 25 minutes or until entire surface is bubbly. Remove from oven and sprinkle chocolate chips over hot surface. Gently swirl melted chocolate chips with knife or spatula to give a marbled look. Cool for 6 hours or overnight before cutting into squares.

Makes about 36 cookies.

Toffee Treasures

2	sticks butter, softened to room temperature	1	cup chopped pecans
1	cup sugar	3	tablespoons milk
1	egg yolk	1	teaspoon instant coffee granules
1 3/4	cups all-purpose flour	2	1-ounce squares semisweet chocolate
1	teaspoon ground cinnamon		
1	egg white, lightly beaten		

Preheat oven to 275°. In a large bowl, cream butter and sugar, with mixer on medium, until smooth. Blend in egg yolk. Sift together flour and cinnamon. Slowly add flour mixture into creamed mixture until crumbly. Spread crumb mixture evenly into a buttered 15 x 10-inch baking pan. Press down firmly. Brush top with egg white. Sprinkle with pecans; press lightly into dough. Bake for 1 hour. In a saucepan over low heat, heat milk, coffee granules, and chocolate. Stir until chocolate is melted. Cut baked cookies into 1 1/2-inch bars. Drizzle with melted chocolate. Cool in pan on a wire rack.

Makes about 70 bars.

Sweet Raspberry Treats

2	sticks butter, softened to room temperature
1 1/2	cups sugar, divided
2	egg yolks
2 1/2	cups all-purpose flour
10	ounces raspberry jelly, jam, or preserves
1	cup semisweet chocolate chips
4	egg whites
1/4	teaspoon salt
2	cups chopped nuts

For color and flavor, use cherries and berries in your Christmas cookies whenever you can!

Preheat oven to 350°. Cream butter and 1/2 cup sugar, with mixer on medium, until fluffy. Add egg yolks; mix well. Add flour, a little at a time, until well blended. Press onto a greased 10 x 15-inch jelly roll pan. Bake for 15 to 20 minutes. Cover crust with jelly; sprinkle with chocolate chips. Beat egg whites with salt and add remaining sugar, a little at a time, until stiff peaks form. Fold in nuts. Spread on top of chocolate chips. Bake for an additional 25 minutes. Cool completely before cutting into squares.

Makes 48 cookies.

Chocolate Nut Squares

Bake with a mixture of salty or tart and sweet, such as sour and sweet cherries, brown-sugar-coated walnuts, and white-chocolate-icing over a crushed pretzel cookie square.

1	stick butter
2	1-ounce squares unsweetened chocolate
3/4	cup all-purpose flour
1/4	teaspoon salt
1	teaspoon baking powder
1	cup sugar
2	eggs, beaten
1/2	teaspoon vanilla extract
1/2	cup chopped pecans

Preheat oven to 350°. In a saucepan, melt butter and chocolate over low heat. Remove from heat and stir in remaining ingredients until well blended. Pour into an 18 x 11-inch shallow pan. Bake for 10 minutes or until done. Cool in pan and cut into squares.

Makes about 48 cookies.

Winter Wonderland Bars

1	stick butter
1	cup graham cracker crumbs
1	6-ounce package semisweet chocolate chips
1	6-ounce package butterscotch chips
1	cup shredded coconut
1	cup chopped nuts
1	15-ounce can sweetened condensed milk

Preheat oven to 350°. Melt butter in a 7 x 11-inch pan. Layer remaining ingredients, in order given, in buttered pan. Bake for 30 minutes. Cool in pan and cut into bars.

Makes 30 bars.

Start a tradition! Bring the family together to have a Nutcracker's Party! Bring in bags of pecans, walnuts, almonds, and peanuts to crack which you will use when baking your Christmas cookies.

Raspberry Meringues

Display your cookies on a pedestal cake stand with glass cover...you know the one that you never use! Tie a big bow on the handle or pedestal.

2	sticks butter, softened to room temperature
1/2	cup almond paste
1	egg
1 1/4	cups firmly packed light brown sugar, divided
2	cups all-purpose flour
3/4	cup raspberry jam
3	egg whites
1/2	cup flaked coconut

Preheat oven to 325°. In a large bowl, cream butter and almond paste, with mixer on medium, until smooth. Blend in egg and 1/2 cup brown sugar. Gradually add flour, a little at a time, until well blended. Pat dough into a 12 x 9-inch baking pan. Bake for 20 minutes. Remove from oven. Spread jam over dough. Beat egg whites until foamy. Gradually add remaining 3/4 cup brown sugar, beating until stiff peaks form. Fold in coconut. Spread meringue over jam. Bake for 20 minutes longer. Cool in pan before cutting into squares.

Makes about 48 cookies.

Wafer Ribbons

1/2	stick butter, softened to room temperature
2	squares chocolate, melted
1	teaspoon salt
1	cup all-purpose flour
1	cup confectioners' sugar
1/4	cup milk
1	teaspoon vanilla extract
1/2	cup chopped pecans

The most enjoyable presentations make a statement of simplicity and beauty!

In a large bowl, cream butter, with mixer on medium, until light. Blend in melted chocolate. Sift next 3 ingredients together and add to creamed mixture. Blend in milk and vanilla; mix well. Stir in nuts. Spread thinly into a greased 11 x 17-inch pan. Bake for 20 minutes. Cut into squares when cool.

Makes about 36 cookies.

Dipped Chocolate Macaroons

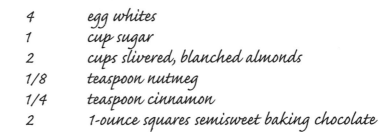

For a heartwarming presentation, use candlelight and holiday greenery with berries.

4	egg whites
1	cup sugar
2	cups slivered, blanched almonds
1/8	teaspoon nutmeg
1/4	teaspoon cinnamon
2	1-ounce squares semisweet baking chocolate

Preheat oven to 275°. In a large bowl, beat egg whites with mixer until foamy. Gradually add sugar, a little at a time, beating until stiff peaks form. Fold in almonds, nutmeg, and cinnamon. Spread batter in foil-lined 11 x 7-inch pan. Bake for 18 to 20 minutes or until lightly browned. Leave in pan until cooled completely. Invert pan; peel off foil. Cut into 1 x 2-inch bars. In the top of a double boiler, melt chocolate over hot, but not boiling, water. Dip one end of each bar into melted chocolate. Place cookies on a wire rack until chocolate sets. Store in an airtight container.

Makes about 30 bars.

Almond Meringue Cookies

1	stick butter, softened to room temperature
1/2	cup sugar
2	egg yolks, beaten
1/4	teaspoon almond extract
2	tablespoons warm water
1 1/4	cups all-purpose flour
1/2	teaspoon salt
1	teaspoon baking powder
1	egg white, stiffly beaten
1	cup firmly packed dark brown sugar
	Chopped almonds

Garnish your Christmas-cookie platter with sprigs of fresh mint.

Preheat oven to 325°. In a large bowl, cream butter and sugar, with mixer on medium, until light and fluffy. Add next 6 ingredients; blend well. Spread into a 7 x 11-inch baking pan. Gently fold sugar into egg white. Spread over dough. Sprinkle with almonds. Bake for 30 minutes. Cool completely. Cut into squares.

Makes 24 cookies.

Butterscotch Bars

Create a holiday centerpiece with a large Christmas candle on a paper doily surrounded by a variety of colorful cookies.

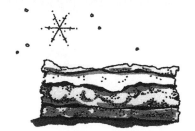

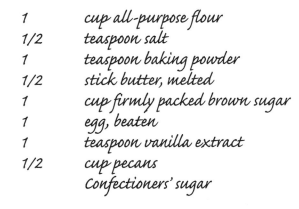

1	cup all-purpose flour
1/2	teaspoon salt
1	teaspoon baking powder
1/2	stick butter, melted
1	cup firmly packed brown sugar
1	egg, beaten
1	teaspoon vanilla extract
1/2	cup pecans
	Confectioners' sugar

Preheat oven to 400°. Sift first 3 ingredients together. Blend butter and brown sugar together in bowl; blend in egg. Add sifted dry ingredients, vanilla, and pecans; mix well. Pour into an 8 x 8-inch baking pan. Bake for 12 to 15 minutes. While warm, cut into 1 x 2-inch bars; sprinkle with confectioners' sugar.

Makes 16 bars.

Christmas Cottage Pumpkin Bars

1	18 1/2-ounce package spice cake mix
1	stick butter or margarine, melted
3	eggs
1	cup canned pumpkin
1/2	cup sugar
1/2	teaspoon grated orange peel
1/2	teaspoon grated lemon peel
1/4	cup chopped walnuts

Cozy up to a warm fire with your family. Share warm cookies and hot cider while playing card or board games.

Preheat oven to 350°. Set aside 3/4 cup of the cake mix. In a large bowl, combine remaining cake mix, melted butter, and 1 egg; blend well. Pat mixture firmly into a greased 13 x 9-inch baking pan. Bake for 15 minutes. Remove from oven; cool. In a large bowl, combine reserved cake mix with remaining ingredients; blend well. Spoon evenly over baked crust. Bake for 15 minutes or until center springs back when lightly touched. Cool in pan before cutting into bars.

Makes about 36 bars.

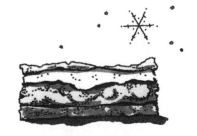

Spicy Apricot Cookies

For a festive look, serve your treats on a crystal or glass platter!

2	cups self-rising flour	1	teaspoon vanilla extract
2	cups sugar	1	teaspoon nutmeg
3	eggs	1/2	teaspoon cinnamon
1	cup vegetable oil	1	cup nuts
1	large jar strained apricot baby food	1	cup confectioners' sugar
			Lemon juice

Preheat oven to 300°. In a large bowl, mix first 8 ingredients until well blended. Stir in nuts. Pour into a well-greased and floured 9 x 13-inch pan. Bake for 30 to 40 minutes or until top springs back lightly when touched. Combine confectioners' sugar and enough lemon juice to make a glaze. Spread glaze over top. Serve warm or cooled. Cut into squares before serving.

Makes about 30 cookies.

Chocolate Walnut Bars

1	18-ounce package chocolate cookie mix
1	egg, lightly beaten
2	tablespoons butter, softened to room temperature
1/2	teaspoon baking powder
1	teaspoon vanilla extract
1/2	cup chopped walnuts

Preheat oven to 350°. In a large bowl, combine first 5 ingredients; blend well. Spread mixture into a greased 9-inch square baking pan. Top with nuts. Bake for 20 minutes or until golden brown. Cool in pan before cutting into bars.

Makes about 12 bars.

Date favorite cookie recipes and store together in a decorative box to pick from in years to come. Add new recipes each year.

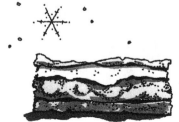

Snow Squares

Serve Christmas cookies hot alongside a bowl of natural vanilla nut ice cream topped with maraschino cherries, drizzled with maraschino cherry juice.

2	tablespoons water
2	tablespoons butter
20	caramels
20	large marshmallows
1	teaspoon vanilla extract
3	cups crispy rice cereal
1/2	cup chopped mixed nuts

In a large saucepan, combine first 4 ingredients. Stir constantly over low heat until smooth. Remove from heat. Stir in remaining ingredients until well blended. Press mixture firmly into a greased 9-inch square baking pan. Set aside until cool. Cut into squares using a knife dipped in hot water. Store in an airtight container.

Makes about 60 cookies.

Lemon Squares

2	cups all-purpose flour
2	sticks butter or margarine, softened to room temperature
1/2	cup confectioners' sugar
4	eggs
2	cups sugar
1/2	teaspoon baking powder
4	tablespoons flour
4	tablespoons lemon juice
2	teaspoons grated lemon rind

For a flavor treat, dip one edge of cooled cookies into melted chocolate. Sprinkle with ground nuts, coconut, or Heath Bar bits. Let cool and harden. Then enjoy!

Preheat oven to 325°. Combine first 3 ingredients well. Pat evenly onto the bottom and slightly up the sides of a 13 x 9 x 2-inch pan. Bake for 15 minutes. Preheat oven to 350°. Combine remaining ingredients in bowl; blend well. Pour over baked crust. Bake for 20 minutes. Cool completely. Cut into bars.

Makes 36 squares.

Berry-Nut Cookies

Heat red-hot cinammon candies in a gallon of apple juice. Serve with Christmas cookies for a flavor treat!

2	sticks butter, softened to room temperature (no substitute)
1	cup sugar
2	large egg yolks
2	cups all-purpose flour
	Pinch of salt
1	cup chopped walnuts
1/2	cup strawberry preserves

Preheat oven to 350°. Grease a 9 x 9-inch metal baking pan. In a large bowl, cream butter and sugar, with mixer on medium, until light and fluffy. On low, beat in egg yolks until well blended. Add flour a little at a time until well mixed. Add salt and stir in walnuts. Pat half the dough into bottom of pan. Spread with preserves. Flour hands and pinch off small pieces of remaining dough. Drop lightly on top of preserves; do not pat down. Bake for 45 to 50 minutes or until golden. Place on wire rack to cool completely. Cut into squares.

Makes 30 cookies.

Almond Shortbread

1	cup blanched almonds	2	teaspoons almond extract
2	tablespoons sugar	1/2	cup sugar
4	cups all-purpose flour	1	egg white, beaten
3	sticks butter, softened to room temperature		

Blend almonds with 2 tablespoons sugar, in food processor with knife blade attached, until finely chopped; set aside. In a large bowl, combine flour, butter, extract, and 1/2 cup sugar. Knead ingredients with hands until well blended and dough holds together. Preheat oven to 350°. Roll out half of dough on a floured surface to form a 12 x 8-inch rectangle. Brush dough with egg white. Sprinkle with half the almond mixture. Use a spatula to press almonds lightly into dough. Repeat with remaining dough. Cut rectangles lengthwise into 8 strips. Cut each strip into 4 bars. Use spatula to place bars, about 1/2 inch apart, on an ungreased cookie sheet. Bake bars for 18 to 20 minutes until lightly browned. Use spatula to place cookies on a wire rack to cool.

Makes about 48 bars.

Gather your family around a cozy fire, sit on comfy pillows, then tell Christmas stories from the past while snacking on freshly-baked Christmas cookies and sipping hot cider.

Maple Butter Squares

Bring Dad and the children in on the Christmas-baking fun! Pick-out recipes together to help bake and, of course, eat this season.

1 1/4	cups graham cracker crumbs	3	cups confectioners' sugar
1 1/4	cups finely ground pecans	1/3	cup maple syrup
1 1/4	cups semisweet chocolate chips	8	1-ounce squares semisweet chocolate, chopped into pieces
1 1/4	cups shredded sweetened coconut	1	cup heavy cream
1 3/4	sticks unsalted butter, softened to room temperature, divided	2	1-ounce squares white chocolate, chopped into pieces

Combine first 4 ingredients and 3/4 stick butter in bowl. Press evenly into bottom of a 13 x 9 x 2-inch baking pan. Chill for 30 minutes. Cream confectioners' sugar, 1 stick butter, and maple syrup, with mixer on medium, in bowl until creamy. Spread evenly over crumb layer. Chill for 2 hours or until firm. Place cream and semisweet chocolate in saucepan. Melt on low heat, stirring to blend. Cool for 20 minutes, or to room temperature. Pour evenly over maple-butter layer. Chill for about 3 hours or until firm. Melt white chocolate over low heat. Cool slightly. Use a teaspoon to drizzle over chocolate layer. Chill for about 10 minutes or until set. Cut into squares. Keep chilled or freeze.   Makes 48 cookies.

Pressed Chocolate Cookies

2	sticks butter or margarine, softened to room temperature
2/3	cup sugar
1	egg
1	teaspoon vanilla extract
2 1/4	cups unsifted all-purpose flour
1/3	cup cocoa
1/2	teaspoon salt

Use frosting to write special messages on your Christmas cookies to your loved ones.

Preheat oven to 350°. Cream butter, sugar, egg, and vanilla in a large bowl. In a separate bowl, combine flour, cocoa, and salt. Slowly add flour mixture to creamed mixture. Fill cookie press with dough. Press cookies onto a cool, ungreased cookie sheet. Bake for 5 to 7 minutes or until set. Use a spatula to place cookies on a wire rack to cool.

Makes about 50 cookies.

Filled Peanut Butter Logs

Gather freshly fallen pecans and walnuts from the ground to use in your cookies!

2	sticks butter, softened to room temperature	2	cups all-purpose flour
1	cup firmly packed brown sugar	1/4	teaspoon salt
1	cup creamy peanut butter	1	teaspoon baking soda
1	egg	1/2	cup crunchy peanut butter
1	teaspoon vanilla extract	2	tablespoons butter, softened to room temperature
		1/4	cup sugar

In a large bowl, cream butter and brown sugar, with mixer on medium, until smooth. Blend in peanut butter, egg, and vanilla. Combine flour, salt, and baking soda; gradually blend into peanut butter mixture. Cover and chill 30 minutes. Meanwhile, make filling by combining remaining ingredients; blend well. Preheat oven to 350°. Fill cookie press. Use a bar attachment to press cookies about 2 inches long onto a lightly greased cookie sheet. Spread 1/2 teaspoon filling on each cookie. Press another cookie directly onto filling. Gently press edges together. Bake for 10 minutes. Use spatula to place cookies on wire rack to cool.

Makes about 30 cookies.

Holiday Fantasy Crisps

1	3-ounce package cream cheese, softened to room temperature
2	sticks butter, softened to room temperature
1	cup sugar
1	egg yolk, beaten
1	teaspoon vanilla extract
2	cups all-purpose flour
1/4	teaspoon baking powder
1/2	teaspoon salt

Let your Christmas cookies reflect the personalities, tastes, passions, and heritage of those in your family.

Preheat oven to 350°. In a large bowl, cream butter and cream cheese, with mixer on medium, until smooth. Gradually blend in sugar. Add egg yolk and vanilla; blend well. Combine flour, baking powder, and salt; gradually blend into creamed mixture. Fill cookie press with dough. Press cookies in desired shapes on an ungreased cookie sheet. Bake for 12 to 15 minutes or until lightly golden. Use spatula to place cookies on wire rack to cool.

Makes about 60 to 70 cookies.

Christmas Trees

Print a Family
Christmas Cookie
Cookbook to give to
friends as a seasonal
gift.

2	sticks butter, softened to room temperature
1	3-ounce package cream cheese, softened to room temperature
1/2	cup sugar
1	teaspoon vanilla extract
2	cups sifted all-purpose flour
	Green decorating sugar

Preheat oven to 375°. In large bowl, cream butter, cream cheese, and sugar, with mixer on medium; blend in vanilla. Mix in flour a little at a time. Fill cookie press, using tree plate attachment. Press cookies onto ungreased cookie sheet. Decorate as desired. Bake for 6 to 7 minutes or until lightly golden. Use spatula to place cookies on wire rack to cool.

Makes about 24 cookies.

Heavenly Vanilla Spritz

2	sticks butter, softened to room temperature
1/2	cup sugar
1	egg, beaten
1/2	teaspoon vanilla extract
2 1/4	cups all-purpose flour
	Decorating sugar

Display the whole cookies on a platter. Cover the broken cookies in a cookie tin to munch on as a quick snack.

Preheat oven to 350°. In a mixing bowl, cream butter and sugar, with mixer on medium, until light and fluffy. Blend in egg and vanilla. Gradually mix in flour, a little at a time, until well blended. Fill a cookie press with dough. Using a star or bar attachment, press cookies onto an ungreased cookie sheet. Sprinkle with decorating sugar. Bake for 8 to 10 minutes or until lightly golden. Use spatula to place cookies on wire rack to cool.

Makes about 60 to 70 cookies.

Cream Cheese Drops

2 1/4	cups all-purpose flour	1	cup sugar
1/4	teaspoon cinnamon	1	large egg yolk
1/2	teaspoon salt	1	teaspoon vanilla extract
2	sticks butter or margarine, softened to room temperature		Colored decorating sugars
1	3-ounce package cream cheese, softened to room temperature		

Preheat oven to 350°. Combine first 3 ingredients; set aside. Cream butter and cream cheese, with mixer on medium, until smooth. Beat in sugar, a little at a time, until light and fluffy. Beat in egg yolk and vanilla. With mixer on low, add flour mixture, a little at a time, until just blended. Insert desired tip into cookie press. Place 1/3 of the dough into press. Press out cookies, 1 1/2 inches apart, onto ungreased cookie sheets. Sprinkle with colored sugars. Bake for 10 to 12 minutes or until edges are lightly browned. Use spatula to place cookies on wire racks to cool.

Makes 60 cookies.

Maple Treats

2	cups all-purpose flour	1/4	cup pure maple syrup, chilled
1/2	cup sugar, divided		
2	sticks butter, chilled and sliced into 8 pieces	2 to 4	tablespoons ice water
		4	teaspoons ground cinnamon
		1/4	cup pure maple syrup

A decorative tassel draped around a silver platter filled with holiday cookies adds a touch of Old-World warmth and class.

Combine flour and 1/4 cup sugar using a mixer on medium. Add butter by the piece, and mix until the dough forms small, pea-sized pieces. Add 1/4 cup cold maple syrup and 2 tablespoons of water. Mix on low just until dough forms a ball. Divide dough in half and form into flat rounds. Cover dough tightly with plastic wrap. Chill for 2 hours or until firm. Combine remaining sugar and cinnamon in small bowl. Flour a rolling pin and board. Roll one piece of dough to form a 10 x 15-inch rectangle. Sprinkle rectangle with half the cinnamon-sugar. Starting with a small side, roll dough up tightly. Dampen edge with water to seal. Repeat with remaining dough. Cover each roll in plastic wrap and chill for 1 hour. Preheat oven to 325°. Use a sharp knife to slice each roll into 1/4-inch slices. Place slices, 1 inch apart, on ungreased cookie sheets. Brush tops lightly with remaining maple syrup. Bake for 15 to 18 minutes or until light golden brown. Use a spatula to place cookies on wire rack to cool.   Makes 48 cookies.

Sugar Cookies

Red and green M & M's added to your favorite Sugar Cookie makes a festive delight!

2	cups all-purpose flour
1/4	teaspoon salt
1 1/2	sticks butter, softened to room temperature
3/4	cup sugar
1	large egg
1	teaspoon vanilla extract
	Colored candies or sugars

Combine the flour and salt and set aside. In a separate bowl, use a mixer on medium to cream the butter and sugar. Add the egg and vanilla, and mix until well blended. Add the flour. Mix on low just until blended. Shape dough into a ball. Flatten the ball; cover tightly with plastic wrap. Chill for 1 hour or until firm. Preheat oven to 325°. Roll out dough on floured board to a 1/4-inch thickness. Use cookie cutters to cut dough into Christmas shapes. Place on ungreased cookie sheets. Decorate as desired or sprinkle with sugar. Bake for 12 to 15 minutes. Do not brown. Use a spatula to place cookies on wire rack to cool.

Makes 36 cookies.

Sugar Cookie Cutter Shapes

1	stick butter
1	cup sugar
2	eggs
1/2	teaspoon vanilla extract
1/2	teaspoon baking soda
3	cups sifted all-purpose flour
	Sugar

Adorn a corner of your kitchen with holiday cookie cookbooks.

Preheat oven to 350°. In a large bowl, cream the butter and sugar, with mixer on medium, until light. Add the eggs, one at a time, beating well after each. Stir in the vanilla. In a separate bowl, sift baking soda and flour; add enough flour mixture to the creamed mixture to form a dough that holds together. Chill for 1 hour. Roll out the dough on a lightly floured surface to a 1/8-inch thickness. Cut into desired shapes. Place the cookies on an ungreased cookie sheet. Bake for 8 to 10 minutes or until lightly golden. Sprinkle tops with sugar. Use spatula to place cookies on wire rack to cool.

Makes 36 cookies.

Filled Chocolate Mint Cookies

When a recipe catches your eye the minute you see it, it probably reflects something you would like to taste!

1	stick plus 6 tablespoons butter, softened to room temperature	1/2	teaspoon salt
		1/4	cup milk
1	cup sugar	1/2	cup sifted confectioners' sugar
1	egg		
2	cups all-purpose flour	2	drops peppermint extract
3/4	cup unsweetened cocoa	3 to 4	tablespoons milk
1	teaspoon baking powder		

Preheat oven to 350°. In a large bowl, cream butter and sugar, with mixer on medium, until smooth. Add egg; beat until light and fluffy. Combine flour, cocoa, salt, and baking powder. Add dry ingredients, alternately with milk, to creamed mixture; beat well after each addition. Roll out dough on a floured surface to a 1/8-inch thickness. Use a 2-inch round cookie cutter to cut cookies. Place on greased cookie sheet. Bake for 8 minutes. While cookies are baking, in a small bowl, blend remaining ingredients until smooth. Use spatula to place cookies on wire rack to cool. Spread half of the cookies with filling. Top with remaining cookies.

Makes about 60 cookies.

Tangy Honey Cutups

6	tablespoons butter	3	cups sifted all-purpose flour
3/4	cup honey	1	teaspoon salt
1/3	cup firmly packed brown sugar	1 1/2	teaspoons baking powder
		1/2	teaspoon ground nutmeg
1/4	cup finely chopped citron	1/4	teaspoon ground ginger
1	teaspoon grated lemon rind		

Place butter in large bowl. Heat honey and brown sugar in small saucepan to a boil, stirring until blended. Pour mixture over butter. Stir until butter is melted. Set aside to cool. When lukewarm, stir in citron and lemon rind. Combine remaining ingredients. Sift about 1/3 of flour mixture at a time into the honey mixture stirring until it forms a stiff dough. Turn out onto floured surface and knead for 2 to 3 minutes. Cover in plastic wrap. Chill for 3 hours. Preheat oven to 350°. Roll out 1/2 of dough at a time to a 1/4-inch thickness; cut into desired shapes. Place on cookie sheet and bake for 7 minutes. Use spatula to place cookies on wire rack to cool.

Makes about 24 cookies.

During the holiday, display ingredients which you will be using often , such as flour and sugar, in cheerful Christmas canisters.

Iced Gingerbread Cookies

Display baskets and Christmas plates for easy reach for when you want to serve your cookies quickly.

1	*14 1/2-ounce package gingerbread mix*
1/3	*cup water*
2	*egg whites*
1/2	*teaspoon cream of tartar*
2	*cups confectioners' sugar*

Preheat oven to 375°. In a medium bowl, combine gingerbread mix and water until well blended. Cover and chill for 2 hours. Divide dough into four parts. Roll out each part on a lightly floured surface to 1/4-inch thickness. Cut into desired shapes using lightly floured cookie cutters. Place on a large greased cookie sheet. Bake for 6 to 8 minutes or until set. While cookies are baking, combine egg whites and cream of tartar; beat until foamy. Gradually add confectioners' sugar, a little at a time, beating until stiff peaks form. Use spatula to place cookies on wire rack to cool. When cool, ice cookies.

Makes about 30 cookies.

Christmas Tea Cookies

1	stick butter, softened to room temperature
1	cup sugar
2	cups all-purpose flour
1/4	teaspoon salt
1	teaspoon baking powder
2	eggs
1/2	teaspoon vanilla extract

Keep a plate of Christmas cookies on your stove with a small scented vanilla candle lit beside them to invite your family to partake.

Preheat oven to 350°. In a large bowl, cream butter and sugar, with mixer on medium, until light and fluffy. Sift next 3 ingredients together. Add to creamed mixture, alternately with eggs and vanilla; mix well. Roll on floured surface to a 1/8-inch thickness. Cut into desired shapes. Place on lightly greased and floured cookie sheet. Bake for 8 to 10 minutes or until lightly golden. Use spatula to place cookies on wire rack to cool.

Makes 60 cookies.

Old-Fashioned Tea Cookies

Decorate your Christmas cookie platters with bright white carnations and red roses or other edible flowers and greenery such as pansies and mint.

4	*cups all-purpose flour*
3	*eggs, beaten*
1 1/2	*cups sugar*
1	*stick butter, softened to room temperature (no substitute)*
1/2	*teaspoon salt*
2	*teaspoons baking powder*
2	*teaspoons vanilla extract*

Preheat oven to 350°. In a large bowl, combine all ingredients. Mix well. Roll dough out to 1/8-inch thickness. Cut with a 2-inch cookie cutter. Bake for 10 to 15 minutes or until lightly golden.

Makes about 48 cookies.

Butter Tarts

2	sticks butter, softened to room temperature (no substitute)	1	teaspoon vanilla extract
1 1/2	cups sugar	3	cups all-purpose flour
2	large eggs	1/2	teaspoon baking powder
		1/2	teaspoon salt

In large bowl, cream butter with sugar, with mixer on low speed, until blended. Increase speed to high; beat until light and creamy. Beat in eggs and vanilla on low until blended. Beat in flour, baking powder, and salt, a little at a time, until well combined. Divide dough into 4 equal parts; flatten each slightly. Wrap dough in plastic wrap. Freeze for 1 hour or chill overnight until dough can be rolled out. Preheat oven to 350°. Roll dough out on a floured surface, with a floured rolling pin. Roll 1 part dough out at a time leaving remaining dough chilled until needed. Using floured cookie cutters, cut out cookies. Repeat with remaining dough. Place cookies, about 1 inch apart, onto ungreased large cookie sheet. Bake for 12 to 15 minutes until edges are golden. Use spatula to place cookies on wire rack to cool.

Makes about 40 cookies.

Raspberry Sandwich Cookies

2	sticks butter, softened to room temperature	3	cups all-purpose flour	
1 1/4	cups sugar, divided	1/8	teaspoon salt	
2	large eggs, separated	1/8	teaspoon baking powder	
2	teaspoons vanilla extract	1	cup raspberry preserves	

In large bowl, cream butter with 1 cup sugar, with mixer on medium, until light and fluffy. On low, beat in egg yolks and vanilla until blended. Combine flour, salt, and baking powder. Beat into creamed mixture. Divide dough in half and form into balls. Wrap each in plastic wrap and chill for 1 hour or until dough can be rolled out. Preheat oven 350°. Roll out 1 part of dough to a 1/8-inch thickness, between 2 sheets of floured waxed paper. Keep remaining dough chilled. Use floured 2-inch cookie cutters to cut out dough. Place cookies, about 1/2 inch apart, onto ungreased cookie sheets. With a 1/2-inch round cookie cutter or donut hole cutter, cut out centers from half the cookies. Beat egg whites lightly. Brush cut out cookies with some egg white; sprinkle with remaining sugar. Bake the cookies 10 to 12 minutes or until lightly browned. Use spatula to place cookies on wire rack to cool. Cool completely. Spread the uncut cookie with preserves; top each with a cutout cookie. Gently press cookies together so that preserves show through cutout.

Makes about 48 cookies.

Walnut Horns

2	sticks butter, softened to room temperature	3/4	cup sugar
2 1/2	cups all-purpose flour	1 1/2	teaspoons ground cinnamon
1	large egg yolk, beaten	3/4	cup finely chopped walnuts
1	8-ounce tub sour cream		Confectioners' sugar

In a large bowl, use a pastry blender or two knives and cut butter into flour until mixture resembles fine crumbs. Mix egg yolk and sour cream in a small bowl. Blend sour cream mixture into flour mixture just until dough pulls away from side of bowl. Cover with plastic wrap and freeze for 1 hour or until dough is firm enough to handle. Divide dough into 5 equal pieces and form each piece into a ball. Flatten balls slightly; wrap in plastic wrap and freeze for 4 hours or chill overnight, until firm enough to roll. Combine sugar, cinnamon, and walnuts. Preheat oven to 350°. Roll 1 piece of dough at a time out on a floured surface to form a 12-inch circle. Sprinkle each circle with 1/4 cup sugar mixture; press lightly into dough. Cut dough into 12 equal wedges. Starting at wide edge, roll up crescent-roll style. Place cookies, point-side down, about 1 1/2 inches apart on ungreased cookie sheets. Form into crescents. Repeat with remaining dough. Bake cookies for 18 to 20 minutes or until lightly golden. Use spatula to place cookies on wire racks to cool. Cool cookies and dust with confectioners' sugar.   Makes 60 cookies.

Place a rich plate of cookies on a table in your entry, for guests to enjoy as they enter and leave your home.

All-Spice Cookies

Give this cookbook along with a batch of cookies baked from one of the chosen recipes as a gift!

5 1/2	cups all-purpose flour	2	sticks butter, softened to room temperature
1	teaspoon ground allspice		
1	teaspoon ground cinnamon	1 1/4	cups firmly packed brown sugar
1/2	teaspoon ground nutmeg		
1/2	teaspoon salt	1	12-ounce jar dark molasses
1/2	teaspoon baking soda		

In a large bowl, combine first 6 ingredients. In a separate bowl, cream butter and sugar, with mixer on medium, until light and creamy. Beat in molasses on low until blended. Beat in flour mixture, a little at a time, until well blended. Divide dough into 4 equal pieces. Wrap each in plastic wrap and chill overnight. Preheat oven to 350°. With floured rolling pin, roll out 1 piece of dough on floured surface to about 1/8-inch thickness. Use large, floured cookie cutters to cut dough into shapes as desired. Place cookies, about 1 inch apart, on ungreased cookie sheets. Repeat with remaining dough. Bake for 8 to 10 minutes or until just browned. Cool cookies on cookie sheet 5 minutes. Use spatula to place cookies on wire racks. Cool completely.

Makes about 48 cookies.

Sugar Bell Buttons

2	cups all-purpose flour
1/2	teaspoon salt
2	teaspoons baking powder
1	stick butter or margarine, softened to room temperature
1	cup sugar
1	large egg, beaten
1/2	teaspoon vanilla extract

A platter of Christmas cookies is a great way to show appreciation to your lawn boy, hair dresser, doctor, etc.

Combine flour, salt, and baking powder in bowl; set aside. Cream butter and sugar, with mixer on medium, until smooth. Add egg and vanilla. Add flour mixture, a little at a time, just until blended. Shape dough into a ball; divide into 4 equal parts; flatten slightly. Cover with plastic wrap. Chill overnight. Preheat oven to 350°. On a lightly floured surface, roll one part dough to a 1/8-inch thickness. Cut out with 2-inch cookie cutters. Place on greased cookie sheets. Repeat with remaining dough. Bake for 7 to 10 minutes or until edges turn lightly golden. Use spatula to place cookies on wire racks to cool.

Makes 80 cookies.

Grandmama's Spice Cookies

To set a more homey buffet table, use baskets, trays, and wooden boxes with Christmas napkins and towels. Serve your silverware and dips in ribbon-tied canning jars!

2 1/2	cups all-purpose flour	1/2	cup sugar
1/2	teaspoon baking soda	1/2	cup firmly packed brown
1 1/4	teaspoons coriander		sugar
1	teaspoon cinnamon	2	large eggs, beaten
3/4	teaspoon nutmeg	1	teaspoon grated orange peel
3/4	teaspoon ginger	2	cups finely ground
1/2	cup honey		hazelnuts

In a large bowl, combine first 6 ingredients; set aside. In the top of a double boiler, over simmering water, combine honey, sugars, eggs, and orange peel. Whisk about 3 to 5 minutes or until mixture is lukewarm. Remove from heat; stir into dry ingredients until blended. Stir in hazelnuts. The dough will be sticky. Cover bowl with a clean towel; set aside for 5 minutes. Roll dough out on a lightly floured surface to a 1/8-inch thickness. Cut out cookies with 3-inch floured cookie cutters. Place, 1 inch apart, on foil-lined cookie sheets. Let stand for 1 hour at room temperature, until tops are dry, before baking. Preheat oven to 325°. Bake for 18 to 20 minutes until cookies are firm and edges are lightly browned. Cool cookies in pans on wire racks.   Makes about 36 cookies.

Crispy Peanut Butter Cookies

1 1/2	sticks butter or margarine, softened to room temperature	1	cup unsifted all-purpose flour	
1/2	cup sugar	1/2	teaspoon salt	
1	cup firmly packed brown sugar	1/2	teaspoon baking soda	
		1/4	cup milk	
1	egg	2 1/2	cups quick-cooking rolled oats	
1	teaspoon vanilla extract	1	12-ounce package peanut butter chips	

Fill a clear glass bowl with scented floating candles. Surround the bowl with Christmas cookies.

Preheat oven to 375°. Cream butter, sugars, egg, and vanilla in a large bowl. In a separate bowl, combine flour, salt, and baking soda. Alternately blend flour mixture and milk into creamed mixture. Stir in oats and peanut butter chips. Drop by the teaspoon onto a greased cookie sheet. Bake for 10 to 12 minutes or until light brown. Remove from cookie sheet. Use a spatula to place cookies on wire rack to cool.

Makes about 60 cookies.

Angelic Chocolate Drops

Bake Christmas cookies to take as a special holiday gift to nursing and retirement homes.

2/3	cup butter or margarine, softened to room temperature
1	cup sugar
1	egg
1 1/2	teaspoons vanilla extract
1 1/2	cups unsifted all-purpose flour
1/2	cup cocoa
1/4	teaspoon salt
1/2	teaspoon baking soda
1/3	cup buttermilk or sour milk (To sour milk: Use 1 teaspoon vinegar plus milk to equal 1/3 cup.)

Preheat oven to 350°. Cream butter and sugar together in a large bowl. Blend in egg and vanilla. In a separate bowl, combine flour, cocoa, salt, and baking soda. Alternately add flour mixture and buttermilk to creamed mixture. Mix well. Drop by the teaspoon, 2 inches apart, onto a lightly greased cookie sheet. Bake for 7 to 9 minutes. Use a spatula to place cookies on a wire rack to cool.

Makes about 48 cookies.

Chocolate Fruit Cookies

1	stick butter or margarine, softened to room temperature	1/4	cup cocoa
		1/2	teaspoon baking soda
		1/4	teaspoon salt
1 1/4	cups firmly packed brown sugar	1	teaspoon vanilla extract
		1	cup raisins
2	eggs	1/2	cup diced dates
1 1/2	cups unsifted all-purpose flour	1/2	cup chopped walnuts

When serving hot Christmas cookies by the fire, throw a handful of potpourri into the fire to enhance the moment.

Cream butter and sugar together in a large bowl. Add eggs; beat well. In a separate bowl combine flour, cocoa, baking soda, and salt. Slowly add flour mixture to creamed mixture. Add vanilla, raisins, dates, and nuts. Chill for 30 minutes. Preheat oven to 350°. Drop by the teaspoon onto a lightly greased cookie sheet. Bake for 8 to 10 minutes or until lightly firm. Use a spatula to place cookies on a wire rack to cool.

Makes about 36 cookies.

In-A-Minute Cookies

Make a big batch of cookie dough, roll it, and freeze in wax paper to use when you need it.

1/2	cup milk
1/2	stick butter
2	cups sugar
3	tablespoons unsweetened cocoa
1/4	teaspoon salt
1	teaspoon vanilla extract
1/2	cup peanut butter
3	cups quick-cooking oats

In a large saucepan, combine milk, butter, sugar, and cocoa. Bring to a boil; boil for 1 minute *only*, stirring constantly. Stir in remaining ingredients; blend well. Drop by the teaspoon onto waxed paper. Let stand until firm.

Makes about 48 cookies.

Butterscotch Cookies

1 1/2	sticks butter or margarine, softened to room temperature
1	cup sugar
1/2	cup firmly packed light brown sugar
1	teaspoon vanilla extract
2	eggs
2	cups unsifted all-purpose flour
1	teaspoon baking soda
1	12-ounce package butterscotch chips

Keep slice-and-bake cookie dough in the refrigerator for quick, last minute Christmas cookies. Sprinkle with confectioners sugar and chocolate shavings.

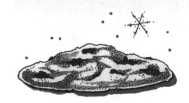

Preheat oven to 350°. Cream butter, sugars, and vanilla in a large bowl. Add eggs; beat well. In a separate bowl, combine flour and baking soda. Slowly add flour mixture to creamed mixture; blend well. Stir in butterscotch chips. Drop by the teaspoon onto an ungreased cookie sheet. Bake for 10 to 12 minutes or until light brown. Cool slightly on cookie sheet. Use a spatula to place cookies on wire rack to cool.

Makes about 60 cookies.

Chocolate Cherry Drops

When you plan to do alot of baking, order in pizza for your family or put on the crock-pot with homemade chili, beans, or soup to make your baking day easier.

1	stick plus 2 tablespoons butter or margarine, softened to room temperature	1/4	cup plus 2 tablespoons cocoa
		1/2	teaspoon salt
		1/2	teaspoon baking soda
		1/2	cup chopped nuts
1	cup sugar	1	cup chopped, well-drained maraschino cherries
1	egg		
1	teaspoon vanilla extract		
1 1/4	cups unsifted all-purpose flour		

Preheat oven to 350°. Cream butter and sugar in a large bowl. Add egg and vanilla; blend well. In a separate bowl, combine flour, cocoa, salt, and baking soda. Slowly add flour mixture to creamed mixture. Stir in nuts and cherries. Drop by the teaspoon onto ungreased cookie sheet. Bake for 10 to 12 minutes or until set. Use a spatula to place cookies on a wire rack to cool.

Makes about 48 cookies.

Peanutty Chocolate Chip Cookies

2	cups all-purpose flour	2	sticks salted butter, softened to room temperature
1/4	teaspoon salt		
1/2	teaspoon baking soda	3	large eggs
1	12-ounce package semisweet chocolate chips	1	cup creamy peanut butter
		2	teaspoons vanilla extract
1 1/4	cups sugar		
1 1/4	cups firmly packed dark brown sugar		

Have a taste test! Gather the family to be the first to taste hot Christmas cookies as they come right out of the oven.

Preheat oven to 300°. Combine flour, salt, soda, and chocolate chips. Mix well and set aside. In a separate bowl, use a mixer on medium to blend sugars. Blend in butter and mix well. Add eggs, peanut butter, and vanilla. Mix on medium until light and fluffy. Add flour mixture. Blend on low until just incorporated. Drop by the tablespoon, 1 1/2 inches apart, onto an ungreased cookie sheet. Use a fork to press gently a crisscross pattern on top of cookies. Bake for 18 to 20 minutes or until cookies are slightly brown around the edges. Use a spatula to place cookies on a wire rack to cool.

Makes about 40 cookies.

Praline Christmas Dreams

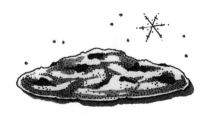

For a special treat, serve your cookies with fresh ground coffee perked with a dash of cinnamon in the grounds.

2	cups all-purpose flour	2	sticks butter, softened to room temperature
1/4	teaspoon salt		
1/2	teaspoon baking soda	2	large eggs
3/4	cup quick-cooking oats	2	teaspoons vanilla extract
3/4	cup sugar	1	cup semisweet chocolate chips
3/4	cup firmly packed dark brown sugar		
		1	cup chopped pecans

Preheat oven to 300°. Combine flour, salt, soda, and oats and mix well. Set aside. In a separate bowl, blend sugars with a mixer on medium speed. Blend in butter and mix well. Add eggs and vanilla; mix on medium until mixture is light and fluffy. Add the flour, chocolate chips, and nuts. Blend on low just until mixed. Drop dough by the tablespoon, 1 1/2 inches apart, onto ungreased cookie sheets. Bake for 20 to 22 minutes. Use a spatula to place cookies on a wire rack to cool.

Makes 36 cookies.

Banana Nut Cookies

2 2/3	cups all-purpose flour	1	large egg
1/4	teaspoon salt	1	teaspoon banana extract
1/2	teaspoon baking soda	1	medium ripe banana, mashed
1/2	cup sugar	1	12-ounce package semisweet chocolate chips, divided
1	cup firmly packed light brown sugar	1	cup chopped walnuts
2	sticks butter, softened to room temperature		

Preheat oven to 300°. Combine flour, salt, and soda. Mix well and set aside. In a separate bowl, use a mixer on medium to blend sugars. Blend in butter and mix well. Add egg, extract, and banana. Beat on medium until mixture is smooth. Add the flour mixture, walnuts, and 1/2 of the chocolate chips. Blend on low just until mixed. Drop by the tablespoon, 2 inches apart, onto ungreased cookie sheets. Dot cookies with remaining chips. Bake for 25 minutes or until edges start to brown. Use a spatula to place cookies on a wire rack to cool.

Makes 48 cookies.

Encourage your teenagers to plan a holiday cookie exchange with their friends at your home. Order in pizza, make popcorn, and watch movies afterwards.

Enchanting Macadamia Chocolate Cookies

Fill a large glass bowl in your kitchen with pictures from Christmases gone by of friends and family.

2 1/4	cups all-purpose flour		1 1/2	sticks butter, softened to room temperature
1/4	teaspoon salt			
1/2	teaspoon baking soda		2	large eggs
1/2	cup sugar		2	teaspoons vanilla extract
1	cup firmly packed light brown sugar		1 1/2	cups white chocolate chips
			1	cup chopped pecans

Preheat oven to 300°. Combine flour, salt, and soda. Mix well and set aside. In a separate bowl, use a mixer on medium to blend sugars. Add butter and mix well. Add eggs and vanilla. Beat on medium until mixture is light and fluffy. Add the flour mixture, chocolate chips, and nuts. Blend on low until just mixed. Drop by the tablespoon, 2 inches apart, onto ungreased cookie sheets. Bake for 20 minutes or until edges start to turn lightly brown. Use a spatula to place cookies on a wire rack to cool.

Makes 48 cookies.

Creamy Holiday Cookies

2	3-ounce packages cream cheese, softened to room temperature
1	stick butter, softened to room temperature
1	cup sugar
2	egg yolks
2	cups all-purpose flour
1	teaspoon vanilla extract
	Maraschino cherries, halved
	Chopped pecans

When wrapping Christmas cookies to give as a gift, tie a cinnamon stick in the bow.

Preheat oven to 350°. In a large bowl, mix cream cheese, butter, and sugar, with mixer on medium, until well blended. Blend in the next 3 ingredients until well mixed. Drop by the teaspoon on a greased cookie sheet. Press cherry and bits of nuts into center of each cookie. Bake for 12 to 15 minutes or until lightly golden. Use spatula to place cookies on wire rack to cool.

Makes about 48 cookies.

Don't Peek Cookies

Your Christmas cookies should include fanciful cookies for children as well as classic cookies for adults.

2	egg whites
	Pinch of salt
1	teaspoon vanilla extract
3/4	cup sugar
1	cup chopped pecans
1	cup mini semisweet mint chocolate chips

Preheat oven to 375°. Beat egg whites with salt and vanilla until foamy. Add sugar, a little at a time, beating until stiff peaks form. Fold in nuts and chocolate chips. Drop by the teaspoon 1/2 inch apart onto foil-lined cookie sheet. Place in preheated oven and turn off oven. Don't look for 8 hours, but no more than 10 hours. Do not peek!

Makes about 60 cookies.

Brown Sugar Holiday Buttons

2 1/2	cups sifted all-purpose flour
1 1/2	teaspoons salt
1	teaspoon baking soda
3/4	cup vegetable shortening
1 1/4	cups firmly packed brown sugar
1	egg, beaten
1	teaspoon vanilla extract
3	tablespoons hot water

To help children celebrate Christmas as the birth of Jesus, let them bake a batch of slice-and-bake cookies formed into the shape of the Cross.

Preheat oven to 350°. Sift first 3 ingredients together; set aside. Cream shortening, brown sugar, and egg in bowl, with mixer on medium, until light and fluffy. Add vanilla and hot water. Blend well. Stir in dry ingredients until well mixed. Drop by the teaspoon onto a greased cookie sheet. Bake for 10 to 12 minutes or until lightly browned. Cool in pan.

Makes 36 cookies.

Festive Pumpkin Nut Cookies

On the front of the Christmas cookie platter, place a guest card with the message "Be My Guest" written in calligraphy.

2	cups all-purpose flour	1	cup canned pumpkin
4	teaspoons baking powder	1	cup raisins
1	teaspoon ground cinnamon	1	cup chopped walnuts
1/4	teaspoon ground ginger	1 1/2	cups confectioners' sugar
1/2	teaspoon salt	1	teaspoon vanilla extract
1/2	cup vegetable shortening	2 to 3	tablespoons orange juice
1	cup sugar		
2	eggs, beaten		

Preheat oven to 350°. In a medium bowl, combine first 5 ingredients; set aside. In a separate bowl, cream shortening and sugar, with mixer on medium, until fluffy. Mix in eggs and pumpkin. Add flour mixture, a little at a time, until well blended. Stir in raisins and nuts. Drop by the teaspoon onto a greased cookie sheet. Bake for 10 to 12 minutes or until golden. Combine confectioners' sugar, vanilla, and orange juice. Drizzle icing over cookies.

Makes 48 cookies.

Pecan Drops

3	tablespoons butter
1	cup firmly packed brown sugar
1	egg, beaten
4	tablespoons all-purpose flour
1	teaspoon vanilla extract
1	cup chopped pecans

Encourage your children to make their favorite Christmas cookies to wrap and give away to their friends at the holiday.

Preheat oven to 350°. Melt butter in small saucepan. Blend in other ingredients until well mixed. Drop by the teaspoon about 5 inches apart onto greased and floured cookie sheets. Bake for 8 to 10 minutes. Cool for 1 minute (no longer) before removing from pan.

Makes about 48 cookies.

Jewel Cookies

Wrap your cookies in festive bow-tied Christmas napkins or handtowels. When the cookies are long gone, a useful gift remains.

2	sticks butter or margarine, softened to room temperature	1	cup chopped dates
1	cup sugar	1	cup flaked coconut
1	cup firmly packed dark brown sugar	1	cup golden raisins
2	eggs	1	cup chopped pecans
2	cups all-purpose flour	1	teaspoon grated lemon rind
1 1/2	cups uncooked regular oats	1	teaspoon grated orange rind
1/2	teaspoon baking soda	1/2	teaspoon almond extract
2	teaspoons baking powder	1/2	teaspoon orange extract
1/2	teaspoon salt	1	teaspoon vanilla extract
		50	candied cherries, halved

Preheat oven to 350°. In a large bowl, cream butter and sugars, with mixer on medium until light and fluffy. Add eggs, one at a time, beating well after each addition. Combine flour, oats, baking soda, baking powder, and salt; mix well. Add flour mixture and remaining ingredients, except cherries, to creamed mixture until well blended. Drop by the teaspoon, 2 inches apart, onto lightly greased cookie sheets. Gently press a cherry half into each cookie. Bake for 14 to 16 minutes. Cool on cookie sheets for 10 minutes. Use spatula to place cookies on wire rack to cool completely.   Makes about 100 cookies.

Old-Fashioned Raisin Cookies

1	cup raisins	2	cups flour
1/2	cup water	1/4	teaspoon salt
1	stick butter, softened to room temperature	1/2	teaspoon baking powder
		1/2	teaspoon cinnamon
1	cup sugar	1/2	cup chopped nuts
1	egg	1 1/2	teaspoons vanilla extract
1/2	teaspoon baking soda		

Enclose a favorite family cookie recipe in your Christmas cards to friends.

Preheat oven to 350°. In a small saucepan, combine raisins with water; boil for 5 minutes. Set aside to cool. Cream butter and sugar, with mixer on medium, until light. Add egg and beat well. Add baking soda to the raisins and stir raisins into the creamed mixture. Blend in remaining ingredients. Drop by the teaspoon onto a greased cookie sheet. Bake for 8 to 10 minutes or until lightly browned. Use spatula to place cookies on wire rack to cool.

Makes about 36 cookies.

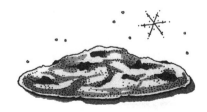

Double Cool Icicle Cookies

Serve your mate herbal tea with a homemade Christmas cookie after he/she has turned in for the night.

2 2/3	cups all-purpose flour	2	sticks butter, softened to room temperature
1/4	teaspoon salt		
1/2	teaspoon baking soda	3	large eggs
1/2	cup unsweetened cocoa powder	1	teaspoon peppermint extract
2/3	cup sugar	1 3/4	cups mint chocolate chips
3/4	cup firmly packed light brown sugar		

Preheat oven to 300°. Combine flour, salt, soda, and cocoa. Mix well and set aside. In a separate bowl, use a mixer on medium to blend sugars. Add butter and mix well. Add eggs and extract. Beat on medium until mixture is light and fluffy. Add the flour mixture and chocolate chips. Blend on low just until mixed. Drop dough by the tablespoon, 1 1/2 inches apart, onto ungreased cookie sheets. Bake for 18 to 22 minutes. Use a spatula to place cookies on a wire rack to cool.

Makes 36 cookies.

Candy Surprise Cookies

2	sticks butter, softened to room temperature	1/2	teaspoon baking powder	
1	cup firmly packed light brown sugar	1/2	teaspoon baking soda	
		1	cup quick-cooking oats	
1	egg	1/2	cup chopped nuts	
1	teaspoon vanilla extract	1	cup candy-coated chocolate pieces	
1 1/2	cups all-purpose flour			
1/2	teaspoon salt			

Surprise your favorite neighbor with Christmas cookies in a festive grab bag hung on the front door. (Make certain they're not out of town!)

Preheat oven to 350°. In a large bowl, cream butter and sugar, with mixer on medium, until smooth. Blend in egg and vanilla. Sift next 4 ingredients together. Gradually add flour mixture to butter mixture; blend well. Stir in remaining ingredients. Drop batter by the teaspoon onto an ungreased cookie sheet. Bake for 12 to 14 minutes or until golden brown. Use a spatula to place cookies on wire rack to cool.

Makes about 70 cookies.

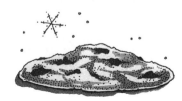

Glorious Chocolate Temptations

Encourage young children to make their favorite Christmas cookies to give to grandparents and aunts and uncles on Christmas Day.

3	egg whites	4	1-ounce squares unsweetened baking chocolate, melted
1	tablespoon vinegar		
1/4	teaspoon salt		
1	cup sugar	1	cup semisweet chocolate chips, melted
1	teaspoon vanilla extract		
1/2	pound ground blanched almonds	1/2	cup finely chopped pistachios

Preheat oven to 250°. In a large bowl, beat egg whites until soft peaks form. Add vinegar and salt; gently fold in. Gradually add sugar, a little at a time, beating until stiff peaks form. Fold in vanilla and almonds. Melt 4 squares chocolate and blend into batter. Drop batter by the teaspoon, 1 inch apart, onto a greased cookie sheet. Bake for 25 to 30 minutes or until set. Use a spatula to place cookies on wire rack to cool. In a saucepan or microwave, melt chocolate chips. Dip half of each cookie into the melted chocolate chips; sprinkle chocolate half with pistachios.

Makes 60 cookies.

Tangy Chocolate Chip Cookies

2	cups all-purpose flour
1/2	teaspoon baking soda
1 1/2	sticks butter, softened to room temperature
1	cup sugar
2	large eggs
1 1/2	teaspoons lemon extract
1 1/2	cups miniature chocolate chips

Holiday cookies look inviting when placed on the hearth or coffee table in decorative baskets lined with Christmas napkins.

Preheat oven to 300°. Combine flour and soda and set aside. In a separate bowl, use a mixer on medium to cream butter and sugar Add eggs and lemon extract and beat well. Add the flour mixture and chocolate chips. Blend on low just until mixture is combined. Drop dough by the teaspoon, 1 1/2 inches apart, onto ungreased cookie sheets. Bake for 12 to 15 minutes on middle oven rack. Do not brown. Use a spatula to place cookies on a wire rack to cool.

Makes 48 cookies.

Cheery Oatmeal Macaroons

Greet house guests with a small Poinsettia, a small bowl of fruit, and a plate of cookies by their bedside when they arrive.

1	egg white
1/4	teaspoon salt
1	cup sugar
1/4	cup grated coconut
1	cup regular or quick-cooking rolled oats
1/2	teaspoon vanilla extract

Preheat oven to 350°. In a large bowl, combine egg white and salt; beat, with mixer on low, until foamy. Gradually add sugar, beating on medium until stiff peaks form. Fold in remaining ingredients. Drop batter by the teaspoon onto a greased and floured cookie sheet. Bake for 10 to 12 minutes or until golden brown. Use spatula to place cookies on wire rack to cool.

Makes about 24 cookies.

Iced Chocolate Cookies

1	stick butter, softened to room temperature	2	cups all-purpose flour
1	cup firmly packed brown sugar	1/4	teaspoon salt
		1/2	teaspoon baking soda
1	egg	3/4	cup sour cream
1	teaspoon vanilla extract	1/2	cup chopped pecans
2	1-ounce squares unsweetened baking chocolate, melted and cooled		Icing (recipe follows)

When you have guests staying overnight, set a small plate with 2 or 3 Christmas cookies on the nightstand for a bedtime snack!

Preheat oven to 350°. In a large bowl, cream butter and brown sugar, with mixer on medium, until smooth. Blend in egg, vanilla, and cooled chocolate. Stir together next 3 ingredients. Add dry ingredients, alternately with sour cream, to chocolate mixture, beating well after each addition. Stir in pecans. Drop batter by the teaspoon, 2 inches apart, onto a greased and floured cookie sheet. Bake for 10 minutes or until set. Use a spatula to place cookies on wire rack to cool. Prepare icing while cookies cool. Spread each cookie with icing.

Makes 50 cookies.

Icing

Keep 2 knives or small spatulas in hot water while frosting cookies. When the going gets sticky, use a fresh, hot knife.

1/2	stick butter, softened to room temperature
2	teaspoons instant coffee granules
2	tablespoons unsweetened cocoa
3	cups confectioners' sugar
1 1/2	teaspoons vanilla extract
3	tablespoons milk

Cream butter, coffee, and cocoa until smooth. Slowly add sugar, vanilla, and milk. Beat until smooth and spreadable.

Chocolate Mint Meringues

3	egg whites
1	teaspoon vinegar
1	cup sugar
1	12-ounce package mint chocolate chips

Preheat oven to 350°. Line a large cookie sheet with a double thickness of waxed paper; set aside. In a large bowl, beat egg whites and vinegar, with mixer on medium, until foamy. Add sugar, a little at a time, beating on medium until stiff peaks form. Fold in chips. Drop meringues by the teaspoon onto cookie sheet. Place cookie sheet in oven. Turn off heat. Let meringues stand in oven overnight. Store in a cool, dry place.

Makes about 60 cookies.

Keep a woven wicker basket in your kitchen with a plastic liner to expose of excess trash during holiday cooking. Keep lemon and orange peels in it for freshness.

Hazelnut Macaroons

Next Christmas party, try wrapping 3 or 4 cookies in pretty tissue with ribbon. Attach a small note with the date and event to hand out at the end as a memento!

8	egg whites
1/8	teaspoon cream of tartar
2 1/2	cups sugar
1/2	teaspoon vanilla extract
1	pound ground hazelnuts

Line a large cookie sheet with parchment paper; set aside. In a large bowl, beat egg whites and cream of tartar, with mixer on low, until foamy. Gradually add sugar, a little at a time, beating until stiff peaks form. Blend in vanilla. Fold in hazelnuts. Cover and chill for 2 hours. Preheat oven to 300°. Drop batter by the teaspoon onto prepared cookie sheet. Bake for 1 hour or until golden brown. Use spatula to place cookies on wire rack to cool.

Makes about 70 cookies.

Raisin-Nut Oatmeal Cookies

1	18-ounce package oatmeal cookie mix
1	tablespoon water
1	egg
1/2	cup chunky peanut butter
1/2	cup raisins
1/2	teaspoon vanilla extract

Keep a small bowl of uncooked cookie dough in your refrigerator for the children to bake or snack on!

Preheat oven to 375°. In a large bowl, combine cookie mix, water, and egg until blended. Stir in peanut butter. Stir in raisins and vanilla. Drop batter by the teaspoon onto an ungreased cookie sheet. Bake for 10 minutes. Use spatula to place cookies on wire rack to cool.

Makes about 30 cookies.

Mini Chip Cookies

1	18-ounce package sugar cookie mix
1	egg
1	tablespoon water
1/2	cup chopped walnuts
1	6-ounce package mini semisweet chocolate chips

Preheat oven to 375°. In a large bowl, combine first 3 ingredients until well blended. Stir in nuts and chocolate chips. Drop batter by the teaspoon onto an ungreased cookie sheet. Bake for 10 minutes or until golden brown. Use spatula to place cookies on wire rack to cool.

Makes about 36 cookies.

Apricot Thumbprints

1	18-ounce package oatmeal cookie mix
1	egg
1	tablespoon water
1/2	cup apricot preserves

Preheat oven to 375°. In a large bowl, combine first 3 ingredients until well blended. Drop batter by the teaspoon onto an ungreased cookie sheet. Press thumb into center of each cookie to make an indentation. Bake for 10 minutes. Remove from oven. Fill centers with preserves. Use spatula to place cookies on wire rack to cool.

Makes about 36 cookies.

Use Christmas cookie baking time to teach your children about how to measure ingredients, break eggs, and pour milk.

Brownie Cookies

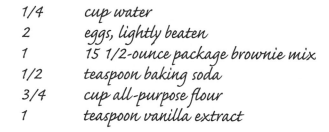

1/4	cup water
2	eggs, lightly beaten
1	15 1/2-ounce package brownie mix
1/2	teaspoon baking soda
3/4	cup all-purpose flour
1	teaspoon vanilla extract

Preheat oven to 375°. In a large bowl, mix eggs and water. Stir in remaining ingredients until well blended. Drop batter by the teaspoon onto a greased and floured cookie sheet. Bake for 10 to 12 minutes or until edges are lightly browned. Use spatula to place cookies on wire rack to cool.

Makes about 36 cookies.

Festive Gumdrop Cookies

4	eggs
2 1/2	cups firmly packed brown sugar
2	tablespoons water
1	teaspoon vanilla extract
1/4	teaspoon salt
2 1/2	cups all-purpose flour
1	teaspoon cinnamon
1	teaspoon baking powder
1	cup gumdrops, cut in halves
1/2	cup chopped walnuts

Don't forget Rover this Christmas. Bake him a dog cookie!

Preheat oven to 350°. In a large bowl, beat eggs until light and fluffy. Add sugar, water, vanilla, and salt; blend well. Combine flour, cinnamon, and baking powder. Gradually blend flour mixture into egg mixture, a little at a time. Stir in gumdrops and nuts. Drop batter by the teaspoon onto a greased and floured cookie sheet. Bake for 25 to 30 minutes. Use spatula to place cookies on wire rack to cool.

Makes about 36 cookies.

Crunchy Banana Cookies

Remember, cookies are the perfect gift. No-one <u>*ever*</u> *outgrows them!*

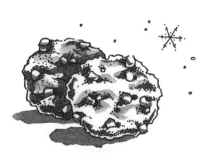

1	stick butter, softened to room temperature
1	cup firmly packed brown sugar
1	egg, beaten
1/2	teaspoon vanilla extract
1	cup mashed bananas
1	teaspoon cinnamon
1/2	teaspoon baking soda
1/2	teaspoon salt
1 1/2	cups all-purpose flour
1	cup granola

Preheat oven to 375°. In a large bowl, cream the butter and sugar, with mixer on medium, until light and fluffy. Add the egg, vanilla, and bananas, beating until well mixed. Add the next 4 ingredients, and stir until well blended. Stir in the granola. Drop by the tablespoon about 2 inches apart onto greased cookie sheets. Bake for 12 minutes or until set. Use spatula to place cookies on wire rack to cool.

Makes about 48 cookies.

Lemon Meringues

12	large egg whites
4	cups sugar
1 1/2	teaspoons baking powder
4	teaspoons fresh lemon juice
2	teaspoons almond extract

Preheat oven to 400°. Beat egg whites until stiff peaks form. Add sugar, a little at a time, until all is incorporated. Gently mix in baking powder and lemon juice. Fold in almond extract. Drop by the teaspoon onto wax paper-lined cookie sheet. Place meringues in oven, cut off heat entirely. Leave overnight in opened oven.

Makes 36 cookies.

Invite Friends and family over and instead of gifts, exchange cookies! Don't forget to include the recipe.

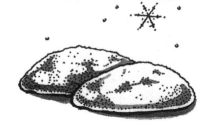

Perky Pecan Kisses

Use Christmas cookiedough as the crust for your next holiday cream pie.

1	cup sugar
3	egg whites, stiffly beaten
1	teaspoon vanilla extract
1	cup chopped walnuts or pecans

Preheat oven to 350°. Gradually fold sugar into beaten egg whites. Fold in vanilla and chopped nuts. Drop by the teaspoon onto foil-covered cookie sheet. Bake for 20 to 30 minutes.

Makes about 24 cookies.

Candied Orange Cookies

1/2	cup vegetable shortening
1	stick butter, softened to room temperature
1	cup firmly packed brown sugar
1	teaspoon vanilla extract
2	eggs
2	cups quick-cooking oats, divided
1	cup diced orange slice candy
2	cups self-rising flour
1	cup coconut

Preheat oven to 350°. In a large bowl, cream shortening, butter, sugar, and vanilla, with mixer on medium, until fluffy. Add eggs and mix well. Combine 1 cup oats and orange candy. Stir into batter. Stir in remaining ingredients. Drop by the teaspoon onto ungreased cookie sheet. Bake for 8 to 10 minutes. Do not over bake.

Makes 48 cookies.

Invite a shut-in over to help you bake. Someone who is unable to stand for long periods can use a bar stool or even work at the kitchen table from a wheelchair. This also offers time for great fellowship and conversation.

Cookies For A Christmas Crowd

Brighten the baking clean up chores by singing Christmas Carols and letting the family take turns.

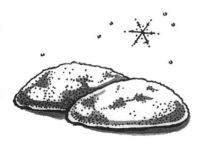

4	sticks margarine
2	cups firmly packed brown sugar
2	cups sugar
2	teaspoons vanilla extract
4	eggs
3	cups sifted all-purpose flour
2	teaspoons salt
2	teaspoons baking soda
6	cups quick-cooking, rolled oats
1 1/2	cups flaked coconut

Preheat oven to 350°. In a large bowl, cream butter and sugars, with mixer on medium, until fluffy. Stir in vanilla. Add eggs, one at a time, beating well after each addition. Sift flour, salt, and baking soda together. Add, a little at a time, to creamed mixture until well blended. Stir in oats and coconut. Drop by the teaspoon, 2 inches apart, onto greased cookie sheets. Bake for 10 to 15 minutes.

Makes 100 cookies.

Soft Molasses Cookies

1	stick butter, softened to room temperature
1/2	cup sugar
1	egg
1/2	cup molasses
2 1/4	cups all-purpose flour
1/4	teaspoon salt
1 1/2	teaspoons baking soda
1	teaspoon allspice
1	teaspoon ground ginger
1/2	cup water

For a striking effect, contrast dark cookies opposite light cookies on the same platter.

Preheat oven to 375°. In a large bowl, cream butter and sugar, with mixer on medium. Add egg and molasses. Beat until blended. Combine flour with next 4 ingredients. Add 1/2 the flour mixture to creamed mixture with 1/2 the water. Repeat with remaining flour and water and stir until well blended. Drop by tablespoon, inches apart, onto ungreased cookie sheet. Bake for 8 to 10 minutes or until golden brown.

Makes about 48 cookies.

Marvelous Maple-Oat Cookies

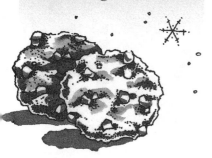

At the annual neighborhood Christmas Party, let the kids cook the dessert, their favorite Christmas cookie, and serve the guests.

1 1/2	cups all-purpose flour
1	teaspoon baking soda
1/2	teaspoon salt
1/2	teaspoon ground cloves
1/2	teaspoon ground ginger
1	cup sugar
1 1/2	sticks butter, softened to room temperature
1	egg, beaten
1/4	cup maple syrup
3/4	cup quick-cooking oats

Preheat oven to 375°. In a large bowl, sift together first six ingredients. Add butter, egg, and maple syrup; beat with mixer on medium until smooth, about 2 minutes. Stir in oats. Drop by the level tablespoon, 2 inches apart, onto ungreased cookie sheets. Bake for 8 to 10 minutes or until lightly browned. Cool for 2 minutes before using a spatula to place on wire racks to cool.

Makes 36 cookies.

Moist and Cheesy Cookies

4	cups all-purpose flour		2	teaspoons vanilla extract
2	tablespoons baking powder		2	large eggs
1	teaspoon salt		1 1/2	cups confectioners' sugar
2	sticks butter, softened to room temperature		3	tablespoons milk
2	cups sugar			Red and green decorating sugar
1	15-ounces tub cottage cheese			

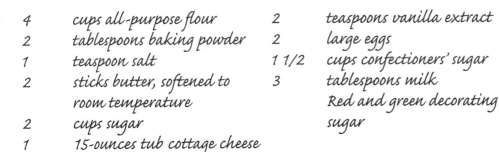

Don't overlook the family attic for a special silver tray or crystal bowl in which to serve your cookies.

Preheat oven to 350°. Combine flour, baking powder, and salt; set aside. In a large bowl, cream butter and sugar, with mixer on medium, until light and fluffy. Beat in cheese, vanilla, and eggs until well blended. Add in flour mixture, a little at a time, until combined. Drop by the tablespoon, about 2 inches apart, onto ungreased cookie sheet. Bake for 12 to 15 minutes or until cookies are lightly golden. Use spatula to place cookies on wire rack to cool. While cookies are cooling, combine confectioners' sugar and milk, stirring until smooth. Ice cookies; sprinkle with colored sugars.

Makes about 60 cookies.

C	is for cookies!
H	is for the helpers!
R	is for recipes worth keeping!
I	is for imagination!
S	is for serving and snacking!
T	is for tasty and tasting!
M	is for mouth-watering goodness!
A	is for after-dinner treats!
S	is for the smiles and the scents of Christmas!

Index

C